FORT SUMTER
NATIONAL MONU

"Where the Civil War Began"

By
Douglas W. Bostick

Charleston Postcard Company

Copyright © 2011 by Charleston Postcard Company
All rights reserved.
First published 2011
Library of Congress CIP data applied for.

Design: Alan Dubrovo
CKI, Inc. BK-CH-10
Printed in Korea

ISBN: 978-1-934987-15-5 (hardcover)
ISBN: 978-1-934987-16-2 (softcover)

Special thanks to Richard W. Hatcher III, Historian for the Fort Sumter National Monument for his suggestions, corrections and recommendations. His insights added measurably to this book.

TABLE OF CONTENTS

Commemorating the Sesquecentennial
of the Civil War in Charleston

Bibliography

An engraving of Fort Sumter by Courier & Ives. *Courtesy of the Library of Congress.*

Chapter 1

Sand Bar Construction

Charleston, South Carolina is located in a natural harbor which provided for a good defense from an attack from the sea. In 1670, the first settlement was located up the Ashley River at Albemarle Point, later changed to Charles Towne. In February 1672, the Grand Council selected Oyster Point, site of the present-day Battery, as the location to which they would move the town. One Council member described the site on the peninsula as, "a Key to open and shutt this settlement into safety or danger . . . very healthy being free from any noisome vapors and all the Summer long refreshed with Coole breathing from the sea." By December 1679, Oyster Point was named Charles Towne.

Entrenchments were constructed and cannons mounted in the new town for defense. In 1696, the colony levied a tax "on Liquors, etc. imported into, and Skins and Furrs Exported out" to help pay for the construction of redoubts and the wall to surround the new town. By the early eighteenth century, the sea wall, entrenchments, parapets, sally ports and drawbridges were in place around Charles Towne.

In May 1707, the Council commissioned a fortification to be built on "Windmill Point" on Boone's Island, later named James Island. This first fortification built outside the walls of the city was later named Fort Johnson, in honor of Governor Sir Nathaniel Johnson. By 1709, James Islander Captain Jonathan Drake was selected as commander and the fort was staffed with a Lieutenant and 12 men. Fort Johnson was strategically placed so that any ship attempting to enter the inner harbor from the shipping channel would have to pass under its guns.

As tensions between England and the Colonies mounted in 1775, the town's Council of Safety ordered the seizure of Fort Johnson, fearing a British naval attack. A second fortification, built of "Mud & Sand, faced with Palmetto Tree," was ordered to be constructed north of the city on Sullivan's Island. This fortification, though not yet completed, was tested early as British Admiral

Sir Peter Parker and nine warships entered Charleston Harbor and engaged the Patriot forces there led by Colonel William Moultrie on June 28, 1776. By nightfall, the British ships withdrew, badly beaten by the palmetto log fort. One British officer wrote, "the Invincible British Navy defeated by a Battery which it was supposed would not have stood one Broadside." This Charleston Harbor battle was the first important Patriot victory of the Revolutionary War. The palmetto log fort was named Fort Moultrie, in honor of its commander in the battle.

After the Revolutionary War, the coastal defenses of the new country were in poor shape. As war was declared between Great Britain and France in 1793, Congress established a committee to study American coastal defenses and appropriated funds to build twenty-one fortifications on the Atlantic coast, later referred to as the "Second System." The forts built in the "Second System" typically made use of earthworks covering wood or brick walls.

In 1797, construction was started on a log and earthworks fortification located at Shutes' Folly, a small island in Charleston Harbor. This island fort was named Fort Pinckney, in honor of the Revolutionary War hero, statesman and presidential candidate Charles Cotesworth Pinckney. The next year, a new Fort Moultrie was constructed over the footprint of the original Revolutionary fort.

In 1807-1808, President Thomas Jefferson, concerned with a possible war with Great Britain, renewed the fortification program, but subscribed to the concepts of masonry forts espoused by French engineer Marquis de Montalembert. Montalembert's concept was to protect the fort's guns by stacking them in covered casemate walls built of thick masonry. Though most building projects were incomplete, none of the First System, built in the Colonial era, or Second System fortifications fell to the British during the War of 1812.

An early map of Boone's Island, later named James Island. Note the notation for Windmill Point at the top right. *Author's Collection.*

Both Forts Moultrie and Pinckney were destroyed in the hurricane of 1804. Fort Moultrie was rebuilt as a brick fortification. Fort Pinckney was also rebuilt, but as a masonry fortification and renamed Castle Pinckney.

In 1816, after the War of 1812, Congress launched its most ambitious defensive system yet, known as the "Third System." In supporting the plans for seacoast defenses, President James Madison offered:

> *. . . whether to prevent or repel danger, we ought not to be unprepared for it. This consideration will sufficiently recommend to Congress a liberal provision for the immediate extension and gradual completion of the works of defense . . .*

Madison appointed a Board of Engineers for Fortifications to inspect potential sites and prepare plans for new seacoast forts. The Board's first report in 1821 recommended 50 fortifications to be built, though by 1850, the list increased to 200 sites on the Atlantic, Gulf and Pacific coasts. The concept for these new defensive forts followed Montalembert's concept of large masonry structures housing guns in covered casemate walls.

The Board of Fortifications was led by Baron Simon Bernard, a French general of engineers and fortification expert from the Napoleonic Wars. The seacoast sites selected were to protect the nation's most important naval bases, commercial ports and harbors. Most of these fortifications were proposed to be built on "chokepoints" of strategic harbors to protect against an attack by an opposing naval force.

The Board of Fortifications sent a four-man team of topographical engineers led by Captain Hartman Bache to survey Charleston and Georgetown harbors after 1821. He was assisted by Lieutenant James Graham, 3rd Artillery; Lieutenant Constant

Mathieu Eakin, 2ⁿᵈ Artillery; and Lieutenant William M. Boyce, 1ˢᵗ Artillery. The region was surveyed in intervals in 1823, 1824 and 1825. By 1826, Bache's team produced a detailed map entitled "Charleston Harbor and the Adjacent Coast and County, South Carolina."

The Board of Fortifications issued a report entitled "The Survey of Coastal Defenses" in 1826, recognizing Charleston as a "first order city." The report recommended that a "pentagonal, three-tiered, masonry fort with truncated angles to be built on the shallow shoal extending from James Island." Construction plans were drafted in 1827 and approved on December 5, 1828. In 1833, the new fortification was to be named Fort Sumter, in honor of General Thomas Sumter, the "Fighting Gamecock," of Revolutionary War fame.

The design for Fort Sumter would provide "structural durability, a high concentration of armament, and enormous overall fire power." The location of the fort would provide an effective crossfire with Fort Moultrie on Sullivan's Island capable of halting any ship's movement through to the inner harbor.

Lieutenant Henry Brewerton was selected as the engineer to oversee the construction of Fort Sumter. Brewerton was an 1819 graduate of the United States Military Academy at West Point. Though only seventeen years old, he graduated fifth in his class. Brewerton's first assignment was to assist in surveying the border between the United States and Canada. He then returned to West Point as an instructor of engineering until he was assigned as an engineer for seacoast defenses.

Brewerton established his base of operations at Fort Johnson on James Island. Work started on the project in 1829 and the first task was to transform a shallow shoal into a 2.4 acre island on which Fort Sumter would be built. Brewerton placed advertisements in 24 New York and New England newspapers for "30,000 tons of stone, in irregular masses, weighing from 50 to 500 pounds and upwards each." He planned to construct a "rock mole" to create a foundation but allow light ships to reach the interior to deliver building materials.

Brewerton signed a contract with a New York supplier to provide the stone at $2.45 per ton, however by 1830, only 1,000 tons of stone were delivered and the contract was voided. Locating new granite suppliers, the construction of the rock mole resumed in 1833. By 1834, 50,000 tons of rough granite was installed creating the rock mole just two feet above low tide.

In the fall of 1834, William Laval, Comptroller General for South Carolina, asserted that he possessed a grant for 870 acres of harbor land that included the shoal under construction to erect Fort Sumter. Despite the fact that the rock foundation was well underway and extensive funds had already been expended, construction on Fort Sumter was suspended until Laval's claim could be resolved.

Further complicating matters, South Carolina was still embroiled in a controversy with the Federal government. Infuriated by tariff acts in the 1820s, John C. Calhoun led South Carolina in asserting that states could address their issues with the federal government by nullifying actions of the government they deemed unconstitutional. This debate extended to the authority of the federal government's seacoast fortification program. Additionally, even though the Fort Sumter project provided a boost to the state's economy, many complained that the construction on the shoal impeded the movement of commercial ships in and out of the harbor.

Laval wrote the project engineer on November 3, 1834, stating:

> *Sirs: You are hereby notified that I have taken out, from under the seal of the State, a grant of all those shoals opposite and below Fort Johnson, on one of which the new work called Fort Sumter, is now erecting. You will consider this as notice of my right to the same; the grant is recorded in the office of the Secretary of State of this State, and can be seen by reference to the records of that office. W. Laval.*

The claim was forwarded to the US Army Corps of Engineers for investigation. On December 8, 1834, Lieutenant T. S. Brown made a report to Brigadier General Charles Gratiot, Chief of Engineers, commander of the Army Corps of Engineers. Brown acknowledged that Laval's claim would appear to cover the portion of the harbor upon which Fort Sumter was being constructed. However, he noted:

> *An actual survey of the 870 acres of low land which W. Laval claims was of course impractical, as much of the water is at times 8 or 10 feet deep, and it is doubted whether the ceremony was gone through with of carrying surveyors' instruments to the nearest sand bank . . ."*

Laval continued to press his claim for the next three years, causing a complete halt of work on the fort. Finally, on December 20, 1837, the Attorney General of South Carolina invalidated Laval's claim. Even though Laval's claim was resolved, the state legislature's Committee on Federal Relations continued to challenge the federal government's authority to build the fort in the harbor.

With a negotiated resolution, work on Fort Sumter resumed in January 1841, under the supervision of Captain Alexander H. Bowman. Like Lieutenant Brewerton before him, Bowman was a graduate of the United States Military Academy at West Point. After graduation, he remained at the school for one year as Assistant Professor of History, Geography and Ethics.

Bowman spent the next nine years as an engineer working on Gulf Coast seacoast defenses, followed by three years working on the Tennessee and Cumberland River systems. In 1838, he was transferred to Charleston.

The rock mole for Fort Sumter, thus far, was only two feet above low tide, leaving the foundation underwater for much of the day. The original plan called for a grill work of timbers to be installed over the stone foundation. Concerned with both proper support and shipworm infestation in the wood, Bowman instead installed a granite foundation to six feet above the high tide mark.

On November 22, 1841, the South Carolina Secretary of State recorded the grant to the Federal Government for 125 acres in the harbor, forever resolving the question of the ability to construct Fort Sumter.

The work on Fort Sumter proceeded slowly. Much of the foundation material was shipped from New England, as far away as the Penobscot River in Maine. While bricks, oyster shell and sand could be obtained locally, they were needed in such quantity that it exceeded the capacity of local brickyards and suppliers. Constructing a fort in the swift current of the harbor presented its own unique challenges. The heat of Charleston summers and the period of yellow fever and malaria, which occurred each year from mid-May to October, were troublesome.

The construction of the island took more than 10 years and $500,000 to complete. By 1851, more than 109,000 tons of stone was used to construct the foundation, walkways and wharf. Construction was halted after South Carolina's secession on December 20, 1860 and the occupation of the fort by Major Robert Anderson and his garrison on December 26.

The fort was five-sided and the outer walls, built of the "best Carolina grey" bricks. Four of the walls featured two tiers of guns in casemates and a third level of guns on a top parapet. Officers' quarters were located inside the fifth wall which only included guns on the parapet. Fort Sumter was planned to accommodate a total of 135 guns, supplied by four powder magazines. The first level was designed for 42-pound Paixhan guns, the second level for eight- to ten-inch Columbiads and the top level for mortars and 24-pound guns.

The parade ground, about one acre in size, was filled with sand and shell.

Bluestone flagging was used for the flooring in the first and second tier gun rooms. Wood flooring was used in the storerooms and in the barracks.

Circular "stair-towers" were designed to be placed at each angle of the fort's walls. Construction on the officers' quarters and enlisted men's barracks started in 1851. The barracks could accommodate six complete companies. The officers' quarters were designed to house the garrison's officers and their families. By 1858, the officers' quarters were relatively complete.

Fresh water was to be supplied by five cisterns, each capable of holding between 4,300 to 5,200 gallons of water. The cisterns collected rainwater fed by terra-cotta pipes connecting to an underground main water pipe.

A wharf, extending 171 feet from the gorge wall, was constructed of stone built atop a grillage of timbers. However, by 1854, the wharf was in disrepair, leaving only 100 feet useable.

By 1858, lack of funds slowed the construction of the fort measurably. With little work taking place, Fort Sumter was used in September 1858 to house 300 Africans awaiting deportation in an incident referred to as the "Echo Episode."

In 1807, both the British Empire and the United States passed laws to abolish African slave trade. The American act, effective January 1, 1808, like the British law, did not abolish slavery but did outlaw the continued importation of slaves.

Immediately, in 1808, the British Navy began patrolling the west coast of Africa to seize and detain any ships engaged as slavers. The ships involved in this enforcement were referred to as the "West Africa Squadron." The United States Navy used a few ships to assist with this patrol beginning in 1820. After the enactment of the Webster-Ashburton Treaty with the United Kingdom in 1842, the United States committed to a vigorous enforcement on the prohibition of African slave trade.

Despite the English and American patrols, the illegal African slave trade was so profitable that many merchants continued transporting captured Africans. On August 21, 1858, the USS *Dolphin*, commanded by Lieutenant John Newland Maffitt, spotted a clipper ship off the coast of Cuba. As the American brig-of-war moved closer, Maffitt read the name *Echo* painted on the rear of the ship. He fired several warning shots before the ship would yield.

Maffitt sent an armed boarding party led by Lieutenant Bradford to the *Echo* where they confirmed the presence of hundreds of Africans. Also, on close inspection, it appeared that the name *Echo* was crudely painted over the name

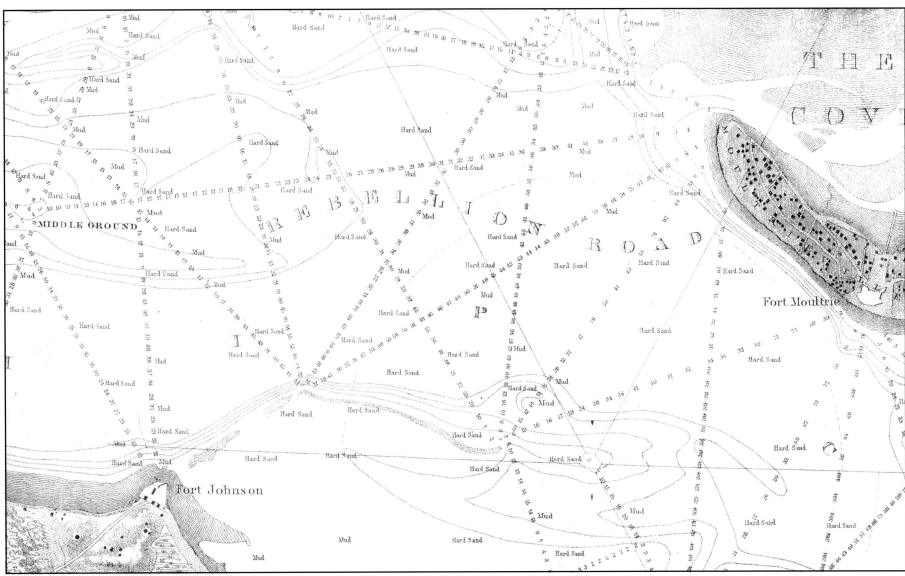

A portion of the 1820s map of Charleston Harbor showing the locations between Fort Johnson and Fort Moultrie. *Courtesy of the Library of Congress.*

"*Putnam* of New Orleans." Edward N. Townsend, captain of the *Echo*, was arrested as was his crew of 18 men. Though the crew included a few Americans, most of the *Echo* crew spoke Spanish or Portuguese.

After inspection, Bradford counted 318 Africans on board the *Echo*. Most of the Africans were boys and some men who appeared to be under 30 years old. He estimated they had been at sea for 35 days.

Maffitt transferred Captain Townsend to the *Dolphin* as a prisoner accused of piracy. The captured crew members were also arrested, but retained on the *Echo* with the Africans. The *Echo*, with Lieutenant Bradford in command, set sail for Charleston. Maffitt sailed for Key West and then to Boston with Townsend. The decision was made to transfer Townsend to Charleston for trial, though many Northerners felt that, in Charleston, rather than be viewed as a pirate, Townsend would "be looked upon as a gentleman who had been a little unfortunate in his business arrangements, but who is entitled to admission into the most respectable society."

Spanish agents for Captain Townsend and his business partners captured the Africans at Cabinda, situated on the Atlantic coast between Zaire and Congo. Initially, more than 450 Africans were boarded onto the *Echo*, though 141 died during the trans-Atlantic voyage. Another 14 Africans died while the *Echo* sailed for Charleston. Upon arrival in Charleston, the Africans were placed in protective custody at Castle Pinckney. They were in poor health from the long voyage in deplorable conditions.

The sheriff of Charleston was pressured by some in the community to declare the arrival of the Africans to be a violation of a state law enacted in 1835 which stated, "That it shall not be lawful for any free negro or person of color to migrate into this State, or be brought or introduced into its limits, under and pretext whatever, by land or by water. . ." On advice of the state attorney general, the sheriff did not pursue asserting his jurisdiction in the matter.

The *Echo* crew was held at the Charleston jail awaiting trial. Federal authorities transferred the Africans to Fort Sumter to further isolate them from the city and the raging debates as to their disposition. The *Echo* was towed to the wharves at the Charleston Custom House where Charlestonians were allowed to tour the slave ship. Charlestonians also booked boat trips to Fort Sumter to view the Africans who were paraded on the grounds as a curiosity.

A large entourage including United States District Judge A. G. Magrath, United States District Attorney James Conner, members of the clergy, several cotton planters, bankers and merchants booked passage aboard the steamer *General Clinch* to visit Fort Sumter. The steamship also transported a bale of blankets, a bale of cotton cloth, a hogshead of bacon and four casks of rice for the Africans. The Charleston *Mercury* reported, "The gentlemen, representing a great variety of interests, were much gratified at the spectacle presented by these savages, who appeared in fine spirits, and entertained the visitors with a display of their abilities in dancing and singing." Their general health improved while held at Fort Sumter, but dysentery was widespread.

Custody of the Africans was transferred to The Society for the Colonization of Free People of Color, an organization that founded the colony of Liberia in 1821/22 as a place to return free African Americans. On September 21, the USS *Niagara* picked up the surviving 271 Africans and transported them to Monrovia, Liberia for resettlement.
Captain Townsend and his crew did stand trial in Federal District Court in Charleston for piracy and murder. Their defense attorney was Leonidas Spratt, a Charleston lawyer who advocated the return of overseas slave trade. In

court, Spratt argued that "revolution must be the inevitable result" if the slave trade laws were not repealed. Townsend and his crew were acquitted since the prosecutor could not offer definitive proof that the *Echo* was an American ship and thus subject to American laws.

Though, with the departure of the *Niagara*, excitement at Fort Sumter subsided, minimal work on the completion of the fort was accomplished due to lack of funding. Finally, in November 1860, 150 masons arrived from Baltimore to complete the masonry work. By December, the fort's walls were complete, but only 80% of the interior was finished and only 15 of the planned 135 guns were mounted.

General Thomas Sumter

Thomas Sumter was born in Virginia on August 14, 1734. He was fascinated with surveying in his studies. After his father's death, he worked in the family mill and tended to their sheep.

Sumter served as a sergeant in the Virginia Militia and involved in the campaigns against the Cherokees in 1761. In May 1762, he accompanied a Cherokee delegation to London to meet with King George III and acted as their interpreter.

He returned to the colonies on October 28, 1762 and wintered with the Cherokees in South Carolina. Over the winter, Sumter captured Baron Des Onnes, a Frenchman sent to encourage the Cherokees to rise up against the British.

Upon his return to Virginia, Sumter was arrested for an old debt, but he escaped and traveled to Eutaw Springs, South Carolina where he opened a general store and invested his money in land purchases. While in Eutaw Springs, he married Mrs. Cantey Gemstone, a wealthy widow, and used her funds to open a second store, a saw mill and grist mill.

Sumter served in the South Carolina militia as a captain. In 1776, he was promoted to the rank of Lt. Colonel with the 2nd South Carolina Rifle Regiment, with whom he served during the critical Battle of Fort Sullivan, the first major Patriot victory of the Revolutionary War.

In 1778, Sumter was promoted to Colonel of the Regiment for the Continental Line. After the fall of Charleston in 1780, he worked to form the South Carolina militia to resist the

British. While Governor Rutledge was in exile in North Carolina, Sumter acted on his behalf in the colony. Rutledge commissioned him as a brigadier general in October 1780.

On August 6, 1780, Sumter defeated the British at Hanging Rock where he destroyed the Prince of Wales Regiment. He faced the notorious British dragoon Lt. Colonel Banastre Tarleton at the Battle of Fishing Creek on August 18, 1780, and the Battle at Blackstock's Plantation on November 20, 1780. At the Battle of Fish Dam Ford on November 9, 1780, Sumter defeated the British and captured Major James Wemyss, the British commander.

During the South Carolina campaigns, a British general remarked that Sumter "fought like a gamecock." The reference stuck, earning Sumter the moniker "The Carolina Gamecock." Lord Cornwallis, whom Sumter tormented through his victories, described Sumter as "his greatest plague." Despite his success in the war, Sumter did not enjoy a good relationship with the other patriot commanders. General Francis Marion frequently criticized Sumter over tactics and the proper rules of war. Sumter and General Daniel Morgan feuded over the proper chain of command for the militia forces.

After the war, Sumter served in the South Carolina General Assembly, the United States House of Representatives and the United States Senate. The town of Sumter, Sumter County and Fort Sumter are all named for him. The mascot for the University of South Carolina is the "Fighting Gamecock," in honor of General Thomas Sumter.

General Thomas Sumter. *Courtesy of the Library of Congress.*

Castle Pickney

Castle Pinckney is located on Shute's Folly, a small island in the harbor channel one mile north of Charleston. In the early eighteenth century, the island was used as a site for hanging captured pirates. In 1746, the island was sold to Joseph Shute. In 1780, Patriot Lt. General Benjamin Lincoln used the island to anchor eight ships that were sunk to create a harbor obstruction for any British ships.

Clinton, both in New York harbor, were similar in design to the Charleston Harbor fort. Castle Pinckney, completed in 1810, was garrisoned during the War of 1812, but saw no action.

In 1832, the South Carolina legislature passed the Ordinance of Nullification

Castle Pinckney on Shute's Folly in Charleston Harbor. *Author's Collection.*

Fears of a naval war between the United States and France in 1797 led to the solicitation of funds to build a fortification on Shute's Folly. The log and earthen fort was named Fort Pinckney, in honor of Revolutionary War hero Charles Cotesworth Pinckney. The fort was completed in 1804, but destroyed by a hurricane on September 8, 1804.

In 1809, the United States Secretary of War authorized the construction of a new fort on Shute's Folly, renamed Castle Pinckney. It was one of only three "castle" design forts in the country. Castle Williams on Governor's Island and Castle

and threatened to refuse to pay Federal tariffs. In response, President Andrew Jackson sent the 2nd US Artillery to garrison Castle Pinckney with instructions to use military force if necessary. They were replaced by a detachment from the 3rd Artillery in 1833. In 1836, the garrison at Castle Pinckney was pulled and sent to Florida for the Second Seminole War. Castle Pinckney fell into disuse and was not garrisoned again until 1860. In 1854, a navigational light was installed at Castle Pinckney as part of the inner harbor directional signals.

With the construction of Fort Sumter, Castle Pinckney's role in the harbor defense was relegated to a secondary role. By 1858, Castle Pinckney served as the powder storehouse for the US Arsenal in Charleston. Its armaments in 1860 consisted of four 42-pounders, fourteen 24-pounders, four 8-inch seacoast howitzers, one 10-inch mortar, one 8-inch mortar, and four light artillery guns.

One the morning of December 27, 1860, when Charlestonians discovered that Major Robert Anderson moved his garrison from Fort Moultrie to Fort Sumter, Castle Pinckney was the first Federal facility seized by the Commonwealth of South Carolina. Governor Francis W. Pickens ordered the Charleston Militia to take the fort. Colonel Johnson J. Pettigrew, commanding three companies of the Washington Light Infantry, the Meagher Guards and Carolina Light Infantry, boarded the patrol boat *Nina* to reach Castle Pinckney. On arrival, they found only one officer, Sergeant James Skillen, Skillen's daughter and several workmen at Castle Pinckney. Anticipating the seizure, Lieutenant Richard Meade had already spiked the guns at the fort. Pettigrew ordered the flag of the *Nina* to be raised over Castle Pinckney, the first time that a secessionist flag was raised over a United States fortification.

Colonel Pettigrew and the Charleston Militia seize Castle Pinckney on December 27, 1861. *Author's Collection.*

In January 1861, the Charleston Zouave Cadets were stationed at Castle Pinckney. In September, Union soldiers captured at the Battle of Bull Run were held at the island fort. The 156 prisoners included men from the 11th New York Fire Zouaves, 69th New York Irish Regiment, the 79th New York, and the 8th Michigan Infantry. When Charleston was evacuated by the Confederates in February 1865, the 21st United States Colored Troops occupied Castle Pinckney.

In 1878, Castle Pinckney was transferred to the US Lighthouse Board and a new harbor light was established there two years later. In 1884, an inspection of Castle Pinckney was undertaken and noted:

> *The fort is in a dilapidated condition; the walls have settled and cracked . . . the gun carriages have rotted away and only parts of the guns are exposed in the rubbish in which they are buried . . . the roofs of the magazines have fallen in . . . that part of the fort which was the barracks is a dangerous wreck, gradually falling to pieces.*

In 1890, the entire fort was sealed and filled with sand. In 1897, Charleston philanthropist Abraham C. Kaufman proposed that Castle Pinckney be established as a home for Union Veterans. Though Congress did appropriate money for the home, the project never materialized. In 1917, Castle Pinckney was transferred back to the War Department and used as a supply base by the US Army Corps of Engineers.

In 1924, President Calvin Coolidge signed a bill designating Castle Pinckney as a national monument and President Franklin D. Roosevelt signed an executive order transferring the site to the National Park Service in 1933. However, in 1951, Congress passed a bill removing "national monument" status from Castle Pinckney and two years later, it was listed as surplus property by the General Services Administration.

There have been several uses proposed for Castle Pinckney since 1953, though none of them have prevailed. Today, Castle Pinckney is owned by the South Carolina State Ports Authority.

Fort Moultrie

In 1775, tensions between the colonies and Great Britain left Charlestonians fearful of a British invasion. Royal Governor William Campbell fled the city and patriots, commanded by Colonel William Moultrie, seized Fort Johnson on James Island. The Charleston Council of Safety ordered "all able-bodied negro men be taken into public service . . . and employed without arms for the defense of . . . Charles Town." The Council also ordered that a fortification be constructed north of the city on Sullivan's Island. Any vessel sailing into Charleston Harbor had to navigate close to Sullivan's Island to reach the inner harbor.

In early 1776, British Admiral Sir Peter Parker and General Sir Henry Clinton planned a southern expedition, culminating in Charles Town. Colonel Moultrie was selected to command a defense force assembled in the city and construction began on a sand and palmetto log fortification on Sullivan's Island. Later, Major General Charles Lee, the American commander of the Southern Department, arrived in Charles Town to assume command. Referring to the Sullivan's Island fort as a "slaughter pen," he urged Moultrie to evacuate the unfinished fort. Moultrie refused and continued to press ahead with the construction at a feverish pace.

By late May, British ships arrived off the coast to scout the channel to the harbor. Most of the British fleet was assembled at the mouth of the harbor by June 8, ready for the attack. The Sullivan's Island fort was still unfinished and unnamed, but did have 31 cannon in place. They were facing a British fleet of nine man-of-war ships with almost 300 guns.

Clinton sent word demanding the surrender of the fort, which the Charles Town authorities refused. At 9:00 am on June 28, the British fleet fired a signal gun to initiate the attack on the palmetto log fort. Despite the ferocious attack and high rate of fire by the British, the sand and palmetto log walls of the fort absorbed most of the shot and shells. Moultrie described the attack as "one continual blaze and roar; and clouds of smoke curling over . . . for hours together." After a nine hour bombardment, the British fleet withdrew unable to destroy the Patriot fort or force its surrender. This action at Sullivan's Island was the first major Patriot victory of the American Revolution, just days before the adoption of the Declaration of Independence.

"The Battle of Fort Moultrie" (June 28, 1776) by Charleston attorney and artist John Blake White. *Courtesy of the US Senate Collection.*

Fort Moultrie, published in Harper's Weekly, 1861. *Author's Collection.*

After the victory, the fort was named Fort Moultrie, in honor of Colonel William Moultrie. The June 28 victory is remembered annually as "Carolina Day," celebrating the success of Moultrie and the 2nd South Carolina Regiment.

By 1798, a new fortification was constructed over the site of the original fort. However, this fort was destroyed by a hurricane in 1804, and replaced by a brick fort in 1809. From 1809 to 1860, Fort Moultrie was home to a garrison of the United States Army. In December 1860, Major Robert Anderson, the garrison commander, moved his men from Fort Moultrie to Fort Sumter, seeking a better defensive position.

Fort Moultrie was occupied by South Carolina troops on December 27, and was a key component in the April 12, 1861 attack on Fort Sumter. Throughout the

eighteen-month Siege of Charleston, Fort Moultrie was gallantly defended, though, like Fort Sumter, reduced to rubble by the rifled guns of the Federal army and navy.

In the 1870s, Fort Moultrie was modernized and rifled cannon and concrete bunkers were installed. In the next two decades, Fort Moultrie Reservation was only a part of the Fort Moultrie Military Reservation as a series of bunkers and batteries were built across Sullivan's Island, including Batteries Bingham (1898-99), Jasper (1899), McCorkle (1901) and Lord (1903).

Through the twentieth century, Fort Moultrie evolved as the United States passed through the world wars. In 1933, Fort Moultrie Reservation was commanded by George C. Marshall, where he oversaw the camp for the Civilian Conservation Corps, a public relief work program. During World War II, the guns at Battery Jasper were replaced by 90 mm anti-aircraft guns. In 1944, the Army constructed the Harbor Entrance Control Post building, a post for the Army and Navy to coordinate the defense of Charleston Harbor. During World War II, construction was started on another battery, east of Battery Jasper, but was never completed.

In 1960, Fort Moultrie and the related building were transferred to the control of the National Park Service and is managed as part of the Fort Sumter National Monument. Visitors to the fort enjoy interpretive displays of Fort Moultrie's history from 1776 through World War II.

A painting by Seth Eastman of Fort Sumter before the war. *Courtesy of the Collection of the US House of Representatives.*

Anderson Moves the Garrison

A *Harper's Weekly* engraving of the delegates and spectators assembled in the South Carolina Institute Hall for the 1860 National Democratic Party Convention. *Author's Collection.*

Issues such as the expansion of slavery into the Western territories and trade tariffs favorable to business interests in the North were fueling the fires of secession by the mid-nineteenth century. English author Charles Dickens wrote of the brewing conflict:

> . . . the North having gradually got to itself the making of laws and the settlement of the Tariffs, and having taxed the South most abominably for its own advantage, began to see, as the country grew, that unless it advocated the laying down of a geographical line beyond which slavery should not extend, the South would necessarily recover its old political power, and be able to help itself a little in the adjustment of commercial affairs.

The 1860 National Democratic Party Convention was planned for Charleston. Southerners were determined to nominate a candidate for president favorable to its interests. Delegates began arriving in the city by April 18 for the convention scheduled to begin on April 23. *Harper's Weekly* described the convention as "momentous . . . and upon the fruit of whose labors the destiny of the Union may depend."

The convention convened at South Carolina Institute Hall with 606 delegates in attendance and 3,000 onlookers crowding into the hall to watch the proceedings. The factions, divided North and South, quickly reached a deadlock over the unconditional protection for slavery in the western territories.

The Southern delegates proposed a platform plank on the slavery issue that stated:

> *Resolved, that the Democracy of the United States hold these cardinal principles on the subject of slavery in the Territories: First, that Congress has no power to abolish slavery in the Territories. Second, that the Territorial Legislature has no power to abolish slavery in any Territory, nor to prohibit the introduction of slaves therein, nor any power to exclude slavery therefrom, nor any right to destroy or impair the right of property in slaves by any legislation whatever.*

Federal Judge Andrew G. Magrath. *Author's Collection.*

The proposal was defeated 165–138 and the Southern delegates walked out of the convention in protest. Anyone receiving the nomination for president had to garner a two-thirds vote of all convention delegates, not just two-thirds of those present and voting. After 57 ballots the convention remained deadlocked and the proceedings were recessed on May 3.

The convention reconvened on June 18, but this time in Baltimore, Maryland. In a fight over delegates' credentials, the Southern delegates again walked out. The remaining delegates elected a new convention chairman and nominated Stephen Douglas as its presidential candidate on the second ballot.

The Southern delegates gathered elsewhere in the city and nominated John C. Breckenridge, the current vice president, as their presidential candidate. This split in the Democratic Party and the emergence of a third party, the Constitutional Union Party, virtually assured the election of the Republican Party's nominee.

The Republican National Convention, held in May in Chicago, nominated Abraham Lincoln on the second ballot. Their platform included a provision to stop the spread of slavery to the territories and the continuance of protective tariffs. In the general election, Lincoln won a majority of the electoral votes and was elected president. Interestingly, with the popular vote split amongst three parties, Lincoln only received 40% of the popular vote.

An engraving of Major Robert Anderson from *Frank Leslie's Illustrated News*, published in November 1860. *Author's Collection.*

Following a long standing tradition, the people of South Carolina did not vote in the election. As in the past, South Carolina's electoral votes were cast by the state legislature and, in this election, they were cast for Breckinridge.

On the night of the presidential election, crowds gathered in Charleston through the night to await any news of the results. Robert Barnwell Rhett Jr., editor of the Charleston *Mercury*, held the November 7 edition of the paper until results were certain. By 4:00 am, the results arriving by telegraph confirmed the election of Abraham Lincoln. The crowd assembled on Broad Street knew that this result would certainly advance the proposals for secession from the Union.

Rhett reported in his election edition, "The crowd [outside the *Mercury*] gave expression to their feelings by long and continued cheering for a Southern Confederacy. The greatest excitement prevailed, and the news spread with lightning rapidity over the city." At noon on November 7, Rhett unfurled a Palmetto Flag in front of the *Mercury*'s offices.

Federal Judge Andrew G. Magrath was presiding over the District Court Grand Jury on Broad Street in Charleston. After concluding the business at hand, Magrath addressed the court:

> *In the political history of the United States an event has happened of ominous import to the 15 slave-holding states. The State of which we are citizens has always been understood to have deliberately fixed its purpose, whenever that event shall happen. Feeling an assurance of what will be the action of the state, I consider it my duty, without delay, to prepare to obey its wishes. That preparation is made by the resignation of the office I have held. For the last time I have, as a judge of the United States, administered the laws of the United States, within the limits of the State of South Carolina . . . We are about to sever our relations with others, because they have broken their covenant with us.*

With his resignation, Magrath became the first paid Federal official to resign his position in protest of Lincoln's election.

Secession fever swept the city. In the minute book of the Washington Light Infantry, a Charleston militia unit formed more than 50 years before, the secretary recorded, "The tea has been thrown overboard–the revolution of 1860 has been initiated."

On November 9, South Carolina Governor William H. Gist, anticipating that the state would secede from the Union, ordered guards to be placed outside the Federal Arsenal in Charleston, "for the purpose of preventing the removal of arms and ammunition by the officers and privates in the Armory in charge thereof." One officer and twenty-two men from the Washington Light Infantry were posted at the armory, the first of any Charleston militia to report.

In acknowledging Lincoln's election, Gist declared:

> *The election to the Presidency of a sectional candidate, by a party committed to the support of measures which, if carried out, will inevitably destroy our equality in the Union . . . the only alternative left, in my judgment, is secession of South Carolina from the Federal Union.*

Following the call by the governor, on November 10, the South Carolina General Assembly called for a Secession Convention to be held in Columbia.

United States Assistant Adjutant General Major Fitz-John Porter was dispatched to Charleston from Washington to assess the condition of the Federal garrison at Fort Moultrie and the construction progress at Fort Sumter. After his inspections and meeting with Brevet Colonel John L. Gardner, commandant of Fort Moultrie, Porter filed his report to Washington on November 11. Of the troops at Fort Moultrie, he noted:

> *The officers–Lieutenant Talbot in delicate health excepted–are in good health, and capable of enduring the fatigues incident to any duty that may be demanded of them. They are sober, intelligent, and active, and appear acquainted with their general duties, perform them with some exceptions punctually and promptly, and all are anxious to give the commanding officer the aid to which he is entitled.*
>
> *The non-commissioned officers and privates appear intelligent and obedient, but do not move with an alacrity and spirit indicating the existence of a strict discipline.*

Porter also reported that Fort Sumter was not yet complete, but a workforce of 110 men was still employed there. Additionally, Fort Sumter's magazines stored 39,400 pounds of powder and a total of seventy-eight guns were located in the fort, but only 15 had been mounted. The barracks and officers' quarters were unfinished. The parade ground was covered in temporary wooden storehouses, sand, masonry, guns awaiting mounting and 5,600 shot and shell. He also expressed concern over the munitions held at the city arsenal but acknowledged, with the presence of the militia guard outside, the impossibility of getting those supplies to Fort Moultrie without a confrontation.

On November 15, Major Robert Anderson of the United States First Artillery received a telegram that he would "forthwith proceed to Fort Moultrie, and immediately relieve Brevet Colonel John Gardner, in command thereof." The telegram was signed "by command of Lt. General Winfield Scott." Anderson arrived at Fort Moultrie on November 19 to assume command of the Federal garrison. It was no small irony that he now assumed command of the very harbor fort where his father was posted and captured by the British in the Revolutionary War.

Inspecting the forts under his command, Anderson took note that at Fort Moultrie he had only two small companies from the First Artillery and nine musicians. Castle Pinckney and Fort Johnson were staffed only by ordnance sergeants and Fort Sumter, still unfinished, was occupied by an engineer supervising 110 workmen, many of them South Carolinians. The Charleston fortifications were designed to confront an attack from the sea. They were not built to defend an attack by land.

On November 23, Anderson made his report to Colonel Cooper, the adjutant general in Washington:

> *I need not say how anxious I am–indeed, determined, so far as honor will permit–to avoid collision with the citizens of South Carolina.*

> *Nothing, however, will be better calculated to prevent bloodshed than our being found in such attitude that it would be madness and folly to attack us. There is not so much of feverish excitement as there was last week, but there is a settled determination to leave the Union, and to obtain possession of this work, is apparent to all…The clouds are threatening, and the storm may break upon us at any moment.*

> *If we neglect, however, to strengthen ourselves, she [South Carolina] will, unless these works are surrendered on their first demand, most assuredly immediately attack us…I will thank the Department to give me special instructions, as my position here is rather a politico-military than a military one.*

In his next report, dated November 28, Anderson wrote of Fort Moultrie, "There appears to be a romantic desire urging South Carolinians to have possession of this work, which was so nobly defended by their ancestors in 1776; and the State, if she determines to act on the aggressive, will exert herself to take this work." He also noted that Fort Moultrie was designed for a garrison of 300 men and Fort Sumter 650 men. Currently at Fort Moultrie, his personnel totaled seven commissioned officers, eight band members, two noncommissioned staff, seventeen noncommissioned officers, and forty-eight privates.

United States Secretary of War John B. Floyd sent Major Don Carlos Buell, assistant adjutant general, to Charleston to meet with the state authorities. After meeting with Mayor Charles Macbeth, Buell reported to Floyd that "all seemed determined, as far as their influence or power extends, to prevent an attack by a mob on our fort; but all are equally decided in the opinion that the forts must be theirs after secession."

Buell also met with Anderson at Fort Moultrie, informing him, despite his small force, Floyd would not send reinforcements to Charleston. He instructed Anderson he was not to provoke the authorities in Charleston, but he was to "hold possession of the forts in this harbor, and if attacked you are to defend yourself to the last extremity."

On December 6, the South Carolina legislature selected delegates from across the state to attend a convention

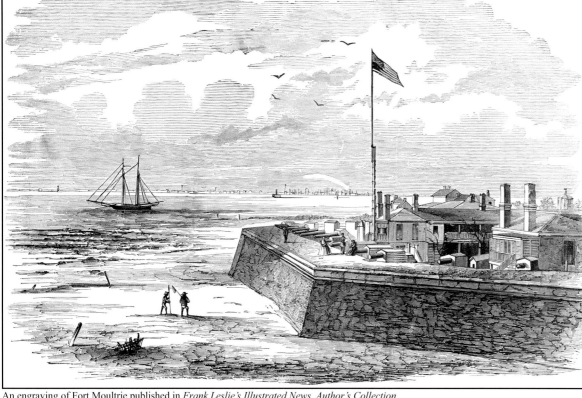

An engraving of Fort Moultrie published in *Frank Leslie's Illustrated News. Author's Collection.*

Celebrations erupted in Charleston when the Secession Ordinance was passed on December 20, 1860. *Author's Collection.*

in the port city, Governor Pickens ordered the steamers *Nina* and *Emma* to patrol between Fort Moultrie and Fort Sumter, both to prevent any additional Federal troops that might reinforce Anderson and to ensure that Anderson did not move his garrison to the stronger position at Fort Sumter.

David F. Jamison, president of the convention, appointed a six man committee to draft "an ordinance proper to be adopted by the convention." The committee, after deliberation, proposed the following ordinance:

> *We the people of the State of South Carolina, in Convention assembled, do declare and ordain, and it is hereby declared and ordained, that the Ordinance adopted by us in Convention of the twenty-third day of May, in the year of our Lord one thousand seven hundred and eighty-eight, whereby the Constitution of the United States was ratified, and also all Acts and parts of Acts, of the General Assembly of this State, ratifying amendments of the said Constitution, are hereby repealed; and that the union now subsisting between South Carolina and other States, under the name of "The United States of America" is hereby dissolved.*

The ordinance was adopted and, after the signing ceremony on the evening of December 20, Jamison announced to the convention, "The Ordinance of Secession has been signed and ratified, and I proclaim the State of South Carolina an Independent Commonwealth."

With the tension in Charleston rising, Anderson expressed his concerns to Washington about Fort Moultrie.

> *We have, within 160 yards of our walls, sand hills which command our works, and which afford admirable sites for batteries, and the finest cover for sharpshooters; and that, besides this, there are numerous houses, some of them within pistol-shot, you will at once see that, if attacked in force, headed by any one but a simpleton, there is a scarce possibility of our being able to hold out.*

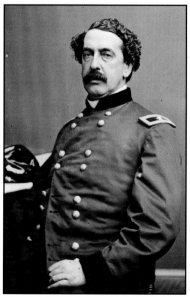

Abner Doubleday, pictured here as a brigadier general, later in the war. *Courtesy of the Library of Congress.*

to consider the issue of secession. One hundred sixty nine delegates were elected to serve at the convention to be convened in Columbia on December 17.

On December 11, Francis W. Pickens was elected as governor of South Carolina by the state legislature. In his inaugural speech, he pledged that the state would "open her ports free to the tonnage and trade of all nations" as soon as she seceded from the Union.

Echoing the sentiment now spreading across the southern states, on December 12, Texas Senator Louis T. Wigfall, in a speech on the United States Senate floor, remarked, "I would save this Union if I could; but it is my deliberate conviction that it cannot now be done…The cold sweat of death is upon it. Your Union is now dead; your Government is now dead…The spirit has departed, and it has gone back to those who gave it–the sovereign States."

The South Carolina convention was opened on December 17 in Columbia as planned. After electing a presiding officer, the convention adjourned to Charleston, concerned about a smallpox outbreak in Columbia. As the delegates arrived

Though he had not discussed his plan with his officers, Anderson began secretly making preparations to move his garrison to Fort Sumter. He ordered Lieutenant Norman C. Hall to charter three schooners, presumably to move the women and children at Fort Moultrie to Fort Johnson. By noon on December 26, two of the schooners were loaded with the families of the garrison and enough provisions for four months. Anderson privately communicated to Hall that the ships were to move toward Fort Johnson but not to land. Upon hearing a signal of two shots from guns at Moultrie, the schooners were to sail for Fort Sumter. Only Hall and Captain John Foster were aware of Anderson's plan.

At dusk, Anderson assembled his officers for a meeting at Fort Moultrie, where he revealed his plans to move the garrison to Fort Sumter that night. He announced to the men, "I can only allow you twenty minutes to form your company and be in readiness to start." Several officers who lived with their families on Sullivan's Island outside the fort had no time to gather their personal belongings.

Captain Abner Doubleday instructed the men on the schooner to remove their hats and coats and hid their insignia and weapons. When the garrison disembarked at Fort Sumter, two shots were fired, signaling Hall to proceed to join them with the women and children. Everyone arrived safely at the new fort undetected. Anderson immediately wrote a report to Adjutant General Cooper stating:

> *I have the honor to report that I have just completed, by the blessings of God, the removal to this fort of all of my garrison, except the Surgeon, four non-commissioned officers and seven men. We have one year's supply of hospital stores and about four month's supply of provisions for my command…I have sent orders to Captain Foster, who remains at Fort Moultrie to destroy all the ammunition which he cannot send over. The step which I have taken was, in my opinion, necessary to prevent the effusion of blood.*

The remaining men at Fort Moultrie spiked the last guns and set fire to the carriages of the guns facing Fort Sumter before they departed. The soldiers arriving at Fort Sumter were met by the workers in the fort, many of them wearing blue secession cockades. Doubleday put the workers under guard until the secessionists were identified and returned to the mainland by boat.

A sketch of Anderson's troops moving into Fort Sumter on December 26 under the cover of darkness. Drawn by William Waud and published by *Frank Leslie's Illustrated News. Author's Collection.*

As the Federal garrison boarded the third schooner, Captain John Foster, First Lieutenant Jeff Davis, the surgeon, Samuel Crawford, and eleven men manned five heavy Columbiads at Fort Moultrie to protect the clandestine movement. Before the Federal troops left, Anderson had them spike all the guns at Fort Moultrie except for the five made ready by Davis and Foster. As they departed Fort Moultrie, Anderson cut down the flagstaff, declaring, "No other flag but the Stars and Stripes shall ever float from that staff."

At dawn on December 27, Charlestonians could see smoke rising at Fort Moultrie. Thinking that the Federal troops were fighting a fire, local authorities sent two fire companies to assist. Word quickly returned to Charleston that the fort was empty and everyone realized that Anderson moved his troops to the formidable Fort Sumter during the night. Governor Pickens was furious with the deception and declared that the move to Fort Sumter was an "act of war." Pickens sent Colonel Johnson Pettigrew and Major Ellison Capers to present his demand that Anderson immediately remove his garrison from Fort Sumter, a demand that was politely refused.

One of the officers at Fort Sumter on the morning of December 27 filed this report with *Harper's Weekly*:

In this engraving published by *Harper's Weekly*, Anderson and his men assemble for a prayer prior to raising the United States flag over Fort Sumter on December 27, 1860. *Author's Collection*.

A short time before noon, Major Anderson assembled the whole of his little force, with the workmen employed on the fort, around the foot of the flag-staff. The national ensign was attached to the cord, and Major Anderson, holding the end of the lines in his hands, knelt reverently down. The officers, soldiers, and men clustered around, many of them on their knees, all deeply impressed with the solemnity of the scene. The chaplain made an earnest prayer—such an appeal for support, encouragement, and mercy, as one would make who felt that "Man's extremity is God's opportunity." As the earnest, solemn words of the speaker ceased, the men responded Amen with a fervency that perhaps they had never before experienced, Major Anderson drew the "Star Spangled Banner" up to the top of the staff, the band broke out with the national air of "Hail Columbia" and loud and exultant cheers, repeated again and again were given by the officers, soldiers and workmen.

Anderson's report of his move did not reach Washington until December 29. On December 27, Secretary of War Floyd telegrammed Anderson: "Intelligence has reached here this morning that you have abandoned Fort Moultrie, spiked your guns, burned the carriages, and gone to Fort Sumter. It is not believed because there is no order for any such movement. Explain the meaning of this report."

The secretary of the Washington Light Infantry recorded his thoughts in the militia's minute book.

News of the clandestine removal of Major Anderson from Fort Moultrie to Fort Sumter, and the destruction of gun carriages, spiking of guns, etc., in Fort Moultrie caused considerable stir among the Citizens and particularly our members, who besieged the office of our worthy Captain until two o'clock, awaiting orders to take the field. At last the orders arrived for our assemblage on the Citadel Green immediately in service uniform, and in an incredibly short time some ninety rank and file were on the ground awaiting orders to march—none knew where—most believing that Fort Sumter was the point of attack. All seemed eager and fully prepared for the conflict, which was expected as a certainty.

Fort Sumter as it appeared before the war.

Legend:
1. Left Face
2. Left Flank, facing Fort Johnson
3. Right Face, facing Fort Moultrie
4. Right Flank, facing the Atlantic Ocean
5. Gorge Wall, facing confederate batteries on Morris Island
6. Left Gorge Angle
7. Right Gorge Angle, where Doubleday commanded a gun crew in the lower casemate
8. Officers' Quarters, ordnance storeroom & hospital
9. Enlisted Men's Barracks
10. Stair Tower
11. Hot Shot Furnace
12. Second Tier Embrasures
13. Fort Lantern
14. Bins filled with oyster shells used in construction
15. Sand and Brick-bat Traverses, built for protection against Confederate cannon fire
16. Sandbag Traverse, built for protection from enfilading fire from Fort Moultrie
17. Machicoulis Gallery, a wooden platform used to drop grenades or fire on an amphibious assault
18. Sally Port
19. Granite Wharf

Courtesy of the National Park Service / L. Kenneth Townsend.

Robert Anderson

Robert Anderson seemed, to some, as an unlikely person to command the Federal forces in Charleston at the height of tension between South Carolina and Washington. He was a Southern sympathizer, though he was opposed to secession. He was pro-slavery and a former slave owner.

Anderson was born on June 14, 1805, near Louisville, Kentucky, the son of Richard Clough Anderson. Richard Anderson served with George Washington at the Battle of Trenton in 1776. In 1780, he was posted at Fort Moultrie and captured by the British in the siege of Charles Towne. Richard Anderson was imprisoned at St. Augustine until he was released in a prisoner exchange. He served as an aide to Lafayette at the Siege of Yorktown in 1781.

Robert Anderson graduated from West Point in 1825, and was commissioned a brevet 2nd lieutenant in the 2nd United States Artillery. He served in the Black Hawk War of 1832 and the Second Seminole War. In 1836, Anderson accepted a position at West Point as instructor of artillery. P. G. T. Beauregard, William Tecumseh Sherman, and Braxton Bragg were among the many students trained by Anderson at the academy.

Anderson married "Eba" Baynard Clinch, the daughter General Duncan Lamont Clinch, a wealthy Georgia planter and retired general from the War of 1812 and the Seminole Wars. In the wedding ceremony on March 26, 1842, General Winfield Scott gave away the bride, standing in for her father.

Anderson served with Scott in the Mexican War and received a brevet promotion to the rank of major. On October 5, 1857, Anderson received the permanent promotion to major of the 1st United States Artillery.

On November 15, 1860, Anderson received a telegram to "forthwith proceed to Fort Moultrie, and immediately relieve Brevet Colonel John Gardner, Lt. Colonel of First Artillery, in command thereof," signed "by command of Lt. General Winfield Scott." He arrived at Fort Moultrie on November 19.

Anderson opposed any war, but he was fiercely loyal to the Union, his oath as an officer and his own sense of honor. In a report to Washington he wrote, "I need not say how anxious I am—indeed, determined, so far as honor will permit—to avoid collision with the citizens of South Carolina."

Anderson was relieved to learn that Brigadier General P. G. T. Beauregard arrived in Charleston on March 3, 1861, to assume command of all Confederate forces. He reported to Washington, "The presence here, as commander, of General Beauregard, recently of the U.S. Engineers, insures, I think, in a great measure the exercise of skill and sound judgment in all operations of the South Carolinians in this harbor."

After Fort Sumter, Anderson was promoted to brigadier general and given the command of the Department of Kentucky, though failing health required him to relinquish that post in October 1861. He retired from active duty on October 27, 1863.

Major Robert Anderson. *Courtesy of the Library of Congress.*

A Courier & Ives engraving of the firing on Fort Sumter, April 12, 1861. *Courtesy of the Library of Congress.*

The First Shot

On confirming Anderson's move to Fort Sumter, Governor Pickens ordered South Carolina troops to take immediate possession of the other fortifications lining the harbor. Three companies of militia, commanded by Colonel Johnson Pettigrew, boarded the gunboat *Nina* to seize Castle Pinckney. They found the fort occupied by Lieutenant Richard K. Meade Jr., Sergeant James Skillen, Skillen's teenage daughter, and more than several dozen workmen. With no other flag at their disposal, Pettigrew raised the flag of the *Nina* over Castle Pinckney, the first secessionist flag raised over a United States fortification.

With Castle Pinckney secured, the *Nina* and the *General Clinch* transported South Carolina troops to Fort Moultrie where the Palmetto Flag flying on the *General Clinch* was raised over Fort Moultrie. It was no small irony that a paddle-wheel steamship named the *General Clinch* took the secessionists to Fort Moultrie given that Anderson was married to the daughter of General Clinch, a Georgia planter, politician and officer.

Pickens dispatched three emissaries to Washington with a letter, dated December 28, for President James Buchanan, notifying him that South Carolina considered the forts, magazines, lighthouses and other Federal real estate now to be the property of the state and urged him to withdraw the Federal troops from Charleston. The president answered with a lengthy letter affirming that he would not withdraw his troops. He closed by asserting, "it is my duty to defend Fort Sumter…against hostile attacks…I do not perceive how such a defense can be construed into a menace against the city of Charleston."

On December 30, 1860, Pickens ordered the seizure of the United States Arsenal in Charleston. Militia troops led by Colonel John Cunningham arrived to find the arsenal staffed by ordnance storekeeper F.C. Humphreys and 14 Federal troops. Humphries, faced with no means to defend the arsenal or its supplies, offered his surrender with the condition that he could fire a salute

An engraving of South Carolina Governor Francis W. Pickens, published in *Frank Leslie's Illustrated News. Author's Collection.*

An engraving of the *Star of the West*, published in *Frank Leslie's Illustrated News. Author's Collection.*

as their flag was lowered. The supplies seized at the arsenal provided South Carolina with enough muskets, rifles and munitions to supply three divisions.

With the fort's interior not yet complete, the entire garrison and families were housed in the officers' quarters. Anderson was concerned for the safety of his garrison and the 43 women and children. His first task was to close a number of openings in the outer wall still not ready for gun emplacements. He requested Captain Foster and his workmen mount the guns sitting on the parade ground.

More than anything else, as a lame-duck president, Buchanan was trying to avoid a military confrontation in Charleston. In a more assertive move, in late December, he ordered troops to reinforce Anderson. Preparations were made to send the USS *Brooklyn*, commanded by Captain David Farragut, with 300 troops from Fort Monroe, Virginia. After further consideration, it was thought too aggressive to send the troops aboard the *Brooklyn*, a formidable man-of-war with 21 guns, and a civilian ship, the *Star of the West*, was chosen for the mission. The speed of the side-wheel merchant steamer might also be an advantage in avoiding fire from the batteries in Charleston Harbor.

On December 31, Pickens received a telegram that Buchanan was going to reinforce Anderson at Fort Sumter. The governor ordered the superintendent of The Citadel, Major Peter F. Stevens, to erect a battery on Morris Island to defend the shipping channel to Charleston Harbor. Stevens recalled students who were on leave for the Christmas holiday and work on the battery began on New Year's Day. Fifty student cadets were posted to the new battery on

Morris Island. They transported 24-pound field howitzers from the school for use at the new battery, named Fort Morris.

The *Star of the West*, commanded by Captain John McGowan, departed New York on January 5, 1861, loaded with arms, munitions, three months of provisions and two hundred new recruits. Assistant Adjutant General Thomas wrote to Anderson informing him of the mission. A workman brought a Northern newspaper to Fort Sumter containing a story about the *Star of the West*. Anderson and his officers concluded that the story was false given that it made no sense to them that this news would be released to the press and that Washington would send a civilian ship rather than an armed man-of-war.

Since Thomas' letter had not yet reached Anderson, in his weekly report to Adjutant General Cooper, he repeated his request for more troops.

> *The South Carolinians are also very active in erecting batteries and preparing for a conflict, which I pray God may not occur. Batteries have been constructed bearing upon and, I presume, commanding the entrance to the harbor…I shall not ask for any increase of my command, because I do not know what the ulterior views of the Government are. We are now, or soon will be, cut off from all communication, unless by means of a powerful fleet, which shall have the ability to carry the batteries at the mouth of the harbor.*

The *Star of the West* arrived at the mouth of the harbor channel at midnight on January 8. Finding the Morris Island lighthouse and the harbor's range lights extinguished, Captain McGowan doused his own lights and waited for morning. He was hoping the South Carolina troops would mistake his ship for a coastal trade ship. At 6:20 am, in a strong wind and cold rain, McGowan ran up his colors and began the high-speed run to reach Fort Sumter.

McGowan's crew could see the flag and battery, but did not spot the cadets at Fort Morris. The guard boat *General Clinch* spotted McGowan's steamer entering the channel and fired signal rockets to alert the batteries.

Cadet William S. Simkins, at Fort Morris, spotted the United States flag displayed on the steamship and alerted his fellow cadets and officers. Major Stevens gave the order to Cadet Captain John M. Whilden to fire on the *Star of the West*. Cadet George E. "Tuck" Haynesworth pulled the lanyard on his gun and fired a warning shot across the bow of the ship.

At Fort Sumter, Captain Doubleday was on the parapet with his spyglass that morning and was surprised to see the Morris Island battery fire on the civilian ship. He alerted Anderson who awakened his troops for action, though none of his guns could reach Fort Morris.

Initially, despite the fire, McGowan continued to move to Fort Sumter. One shot struck the ship near the rudder and a second shot struck about two feet above the water line. Taking on effective fire from Fort Morris and with the guns at Fort Moultrie now engaged, McGowan turned his ship to leave the harbor without reinforcing Anderson.

In this *Harper's Weekly* engraving, Citadel cadets are firing on the *Star of the West*, attempting to reinforce and re-supply Fort Sumter. *Author's Collection.*

As captured in this *Harper's Weekly* engraving, the families depart Fort Sumter on February 3, 1861. *Author's Collection.*

An engraving of Brigadier General P. G. T. Beauregard published in *Frank Leslie's Illustrated News. Author's Collection.*

Anderson was incensed over the firing on the *Star of the West* and immediately sent a letter of protest to Pickens, to which he responded, "The act is perfectly justified by me." Pickens then ordered the seizure of the *Marion*, an eight-hundred-ton steamship that provided cargo and passenger service between New York and Charleston, and had it converted to a man-of-war to patrol the harbor and shipping channel should another attempt be made to resupply Anderson and his garrison.

The next day, the *Mercury* published an editorial about the attempt to reinforce Fort Sumter.

Yesterday, the ninth of January, will be remembered in history. Powder has been burnt over the decree of our State, timber has been crashed, perhaps blood spilled. The expulsion of the "Star of the West" from Charleston Harbor yesterday morning was the opening of the ball of Revolution. We are proud that our harbor has been so honored. We are proud that the State of South Carolina, so long, so bitterly, and so contemptuously reviled and scoffed at, above all others, should thus proudly have thrown back the scoff of her enemies. Entrenched upon her soil, she has spoken from the mouth of her cannon, and not from the mouths of scurrilous demagogues, fanatics, and scribblers…South Carolina will stand under her own Palmetto tree, unterrified by the snarling growls or assaults of the one, undeceived or deterred by the wily machinations of the other. And if that red seal of blood be still lacking for the parchment of our liberties, and blood they want–blood they shall have–and blood enough to stamp it all in red. For, by the God of our Fathers, the soil of South Carolina shall be free!

Despite the *Star of the West* incident, Pickens decided to allow the resumption of mail service to and from Fort Sumter and agreed to receive orders from Anderson for provisions and deliver them to the fort. Washington was notified that "Major Anderson and his command do now obtain all necessary supplies, including fresh meat and vegetables, and, I believe, fuel and water, from the city of Charleston, and do now enjoy communication by post and special messenger with the President, and will continue to do so, certainly until the door to negotiation has been closed."

As tensions continued to mount, Anderson grew concerned about the presence of women and children in Fort Sumter. On January 21, he received permission from Pickens to evacuate the families to New York. On February 3, the *Marion* was pulled from patrol duty and picked up the women and children at Fort Sumter. One of the departing wives wrote:

When the ship was passing, [the fort] fired a gun and gave three heart-thrilling cheers as a parting farewell to the dear loved ones on board, whom they may possibly never meet again this side of the grave. The response was weeping and waving adieux to husbands and fathers. A small band put up in an isolated fort, completely surrounded by instruments of death, as five forts could be seen from the steamer's deck, with their guns pointing toward Sumter.

On January 28, 1861, South Carolina formally adopted the palmetto flag with a blue field and a white crescent in the top, left corner as the official state flag. A red version of this flag was flown earlier by Citadel cadets at Fort Morris.

By early February, Mississippi, Florida, Alabama, Georgia, Louisiana and Texas joined South Carolina in seceding from the Union. Each state sent delegates to meet in convention in Montgomery, Alabama, and on February 8, the Confederate States of America was formed. Former US Senator Jefferson Davis of Mississippi was elected as president. Concerned that Pickens would act impulsively and prematurely, Davis informed the South Carolina governor that any decisions regarding Fort Sumter were now the responsibility of the Confederate government.

On instructions of the Montgomery convention, Confederate Secretary of War Leroy P. Walker telegrammed Pickens on March 1: "This government assumes the control of the military operations at Charleston and will make demand of the fort when fully advised. An officer goes tonight to take charge." Davis appointed P. G. T. Beauregard to the rank of brigadier general in the Provisional Army of the Confederate States, making him the first appointment to general by the new president, and dispatched him to Charleston.

Ward Lamon, a close personal friend of Abraham Lincoln. *Courtesy of the Library of Congress.*

Beauregard arrived in Charleston on March 3, 1861, to accept command of all forces there. Beauregard's favorite professor at West Point was Robert Anderson. The two men shared a great affection for each other. When Anderson learned that his former student was in command, he wrote to Washington on March 6, noting, "The presence here, as commander, of General Beauregard, recently of the U.S. Engineers, insures, I think, in a great measure the exercise of skill and sound judgment in all operations of the South Carolinians in this harbor." He ended his letter with, "God grant that our country may be saved from the horrors of a fratricidal war!" The stage was now set between Beauregard and Anderson—student and teacher, two experts in artillery, two men with great devotion to honor.

Stephen A. Hurlbut, a personal friend of Abraham Lincoln, formerly served as an officer for a South Carolina infantry regiment in the Second Seminole War. *Courtesy of the Library of Congress.*

Beauregard was not satisfied with the defenses at Charleston. He began further preparations in the city to defend an attack from the sea and place an effective ring of batteries around Fort Sumter.

The day after Beauregard arrived in Charleston, Lincoln was inaugurated in Washington. In his inauguration speech, he stated:

> *I am loath to close. We are not enemies, but friends. We must not be enemies. Though passion may have strained, it must not break our bonds of affection. The mystic chords of memory, stretching from every battlefield, and patriot grave, to every living heart and hearthstone, all over this broad land, will yet swell the chorus of the Union, when again touched, as surely they will be, by the better angels of our nature.*

Lincoln was clear that he regarded secession as illegal and that he intended to maintain possession of all federal property, including munitions and fortifications, in the states that had seceded.

Given Lincoln's resolve, the Confederate War Department expected him to take action quickly. Confederate Secretary of War Walker wrote Beauregard on March 9:

> *Fort Sumter is silent now only because of the weakness of the garrison. Should re-enforcements get in, her guns would open fire on you. There is information at this Department–not official, it is true, but believed to be reliable–that five or six United States ships are in New York Harbor all ready to start. The United States steamer "Pawnee" has left Philadelphia suddenly for Washington, fully provisioned and ready to go to sea, and it is probable that the effort to re-enforce Sumter may be made by sending in men in whale-boats.*

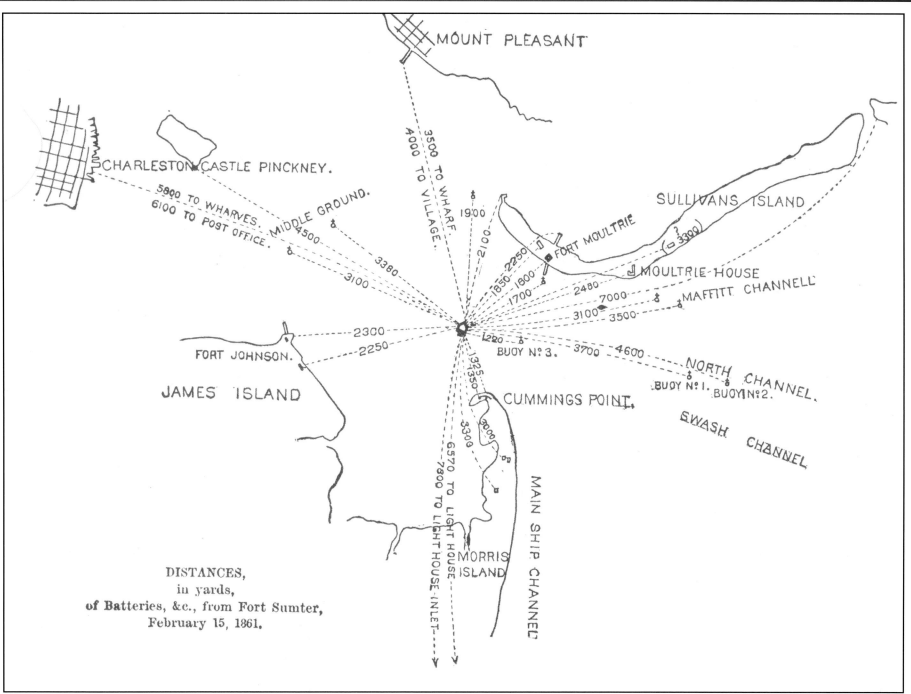

MOUNT PLEASANT

CHARLESTON CASTLE PINCKNEY.

SULLIVANS ISLAND

MIDDLE GROUND.

5900 TO WHARVES.
6100 TO POST OFFICE.

4500

3380

3100

3500 TO WHARF.
4000 TO VILLAGE.

1900

2100

2250

1850 1800

1700

FORT MOULTRIE

(= 3300)

MOULTRIE HOUSE

2480

7000

MAFFITT CHANNELL

3100 3500

2300

2250

FORT JOHNSON.

JAMES ISLAND

1220

1325 1350

BUOY Nº 3.

3700 4600

NORTH CHANNEL.

CUMMINGS POINT.

BUOY Nº 1. BUOY Nº 2.

SWASH CHANNEL

3000

3300

6570 TO LIGHT HOUSE
7800 TO LIGHT HOUSE INLET

MORRIS ISLAND

MAIN SHIP CHANNEL

DISTANCES,
in yards,
of Batteries, &c., from Fort Sumter,
February 15, 1861.

This map, drawn by an officer at Fort Sumter, marked the distances to Confederate batteries and landmarks surrounding the fort. *Courtesy of the Library of Congress.*

FORT SUMTER NATIONAL MONUMENT "Where the Civil War Began"

On March 13, Captain Gustavus V. Fox, a trusted friend of the president, met with Lincoln to propose a naval expedition to reinforce Fort Sumter. Lincoln did not act immediately, but he did send Fox to Charleston to meet with Anderson. While Anderson did not favor Fox's plan, he did send word to the president that he could not hold out past mid-April.

On March 21, Lincoln sent two other close friends to Charleston: Ward Lamon, a former law partner, and Stephen Hurlbut, an Illinois attorney and Charleston native. Lamon met with Pickens and the governor instructed him that "nothing can prevent war except acquiescence of the President of the United States in secession, and his unalterable resolve not to attempt any reinforcements of the Southern forts." Lamon assured Pickens that there would be no attempt to reinforce Anderson and he believed Fort Sumter would likely be abandoned.

Lamon next visited with Anderson at Fort Sumter where he was advised that the fort was low on provisions, which consisted only of six barrels of flour, six barrels of hard bread, three barrels of sugar, one barrel of coffee, two barrels of vinegar, twenty-six barrels of pork, one quarter barrel of salt, one and a half barrels of rice and three boxes of candles. Lamon would later write that he was sent on a mission by the president to "the virtual capital of the state which had been the pioneer in all of this haughty and stupendous work of rebellion."

Hurlbut, after meeting with relatives and contacts in Charlestonians, reported to Lincoln:

> I have no hesitation in reporting as unquestionable, that Separate Nationality is a fixed fact, that there is an unanimity of sentiment which to my mind is astonishing–that there is no attachment to the Union–that almost every one of those very men who in 1832 held military commissions under secret orders from General Jackson and in fact were ready to draw the sword in civil war for the nation, are now as ready to take arms if necessary for the Southern Confederacy . . . They expect a Golden age, when Charleston shall be a great Commercial Emporium and Control for the South as New York does for the North.

Anderson, tired of being penned up in Fort Sumter, expressed that he felt like he was "a sheep tied, watching the butcher sharpening a knife to cut his throat . . . I must say that I think the Government has left me too much to myself–has not given me instructions, even when I asked for them."

On April 4, Lincoln met again with Captain Fox, but this time accepted his proposal for a naval expedition and reinforcement of Fort Sumter. He told Fox,

however, that he would notify both Anderson and Governor Pickens. The notice to Anderson, written by the president but signed by Secretary of War Simon Cameron, read:

> Sir: Your letter of the 1st instant occasions some anxiety to the President. On the information of Captain Fox he had supposed you could hold out till the 15th instant without any great inconvenience; and had prepared an expedition to relieve you before that period. Hoping that you will be able to sustain yourself till the 11th or 12th instant, the expedition will go forward; and, finding your flag flying, will attempt to provision you, and, in case the effort is resisted, will endeavor also to reinforce you. You will therefore hold out, if possible, till the arrival of the expedition. It is not, however, the intention of the President to subject your command to any danger or hardship beyond what, in your judgment, would be usual in military life; and he has entire confidence that you will act as becomes a patriot and soldier, under the circumstances. Whenever, if at all, in your judgment, to save yourself and command, a capitulation becomes a necessity, you are authorized to make it.

On April 6, Lincoln sent an unsigned, unaddressed message to Pickens for personal delivery by Robert Chew, a trusted State Department clerk. The note read:

> I am directed by the President of the United States to notify you to expect an attempt will be made to supply Fort Sumter with provisions only; and that, if such an attempt be not resisted, no effort to throw in men, arms, or ammunition will be made without further notice, or in case of an attack by upon the fort.

The naval ships were assembled in New York by Fox to sail to Fort Sumter. Lincoln sent his own sealed orders to the USS *Powhatan*, the most formidable ship of the group. Unknown even to Fox, the *Powhatan* was to sail, not to Fort Sumter but to Fort Pickens in Florida.

The USS *Pawnee*, USS *Pocahontas*, USS *Harriet Lane* and two transports under the command of Captain Fox did set sail for Charleston, thinking that the *Powhatan* was headed to the same destination. On April 6, authorities in Charleston received a telegram from Washington simply signed "A Friend," informing them that an armed expedition was en route to Fort Sumter.

Beauregard immediately stopped all supply deliveries and mail service for Fort Sumter. At the post office, Confederate officers seized two official letters

A National Park Service diorama of the Beach Battery at Fort Johnson firing the first shot over Fort Sumter on April 12, 1861. *Photograph taken by Bryan Riggs.*

from Sumter, one written by Anderson and the other by Foster. Opening the Anderson report, Beauregard and Pickens were surprised to learn that supplies at the fort were extremely low. Anderson also indicated that based on Lamon's remarks in March, he was shocked to hear that an expedition was now en route. Anderson expressed, "We shall strive to do our duty, though I frankly say that my heart is not in this war which I see is to be thus commenced."

Beauregard notified Anderson, "I have the honor to inform you that, in consequence of the delays and apparent vacillations of the United States Government at Washington relative to the evacuation of Fort Sumter, no further communications…will be permitted." Confederate Secretary of War Walker telegrammed Beauregard, "Under no circumstance are you to allow provisions to be sent to Fort Sumter." On April 10, Davis wired Beauregard to demand the evacuation of the fort and attack if refused.

Private Thompson, stationed with Anderson at Fort Sumter, recorded in his journal:

> *Our supply of breadstuffs was fast giving out, and the Carolinians knew it. They had cut off all communication with the shore, and starvation was staring us in the face. We had been on ¾ rations for a long time and on the 8th of April a reduction to half rations was made and cheerfully submitted to, the hope of being re-enforced or withdrawn having not yet entirely left us. On the eleventh one biscuit was our allowance, and matters seemed rapidly coming to a crisis.*

On the afternoon of April 11, Beauregard sent Colonel James Chesnut Jr. and Captain Stephen Dill Lee to Fort Sumter to deliver a message. The letter delivered an ultimatum to Anderson:

> *I am ordered by the Government of the Confederate States to demand the evacuation of Fort Sumter. My aides, Colonel Chestnut and Captain Lee, are authorized to make such demand of you. All proper facilities will be afforded for the removal of yourself and command, together with company arms and property, and all private property, to any post in the United States which you may select. The flag which you have upheld so long and with so much fortitude, under the most trying circumstances, may be saluted by you on taking it down.*

After conferring with his officers, Anderson responded to Beauregard:

> *General: I have the honor to acknowledge the receipt of your com-*

This engraving was published on the front page of *Harper's Weekly* announcing the April 12, 1861, firing on Fort Sumter. *Author's Collection.*

> *munication demanding the evacuation of this fort, and to say, in reply thereto, that it is a demand with which I regret that my sense of honor, and of my obligations to my Government, prevent my compliance. Thanking you for the fair, manly and courteous terms proposed, and for the high compliment paid me, I am, very respectfully,*
> *Your Obedient Servant,*
> *Robert Anderson, Major, First Artillery, Commanding*

On the night of April 11, lookouts spotted the masts of the Federal ships forming offshore. Anderson informed Beauregard's aides that he would agree to evacuate the fort on April 15, provided that he received no further instructions or supplies from Washington. Knowing of the arrival of the Federal ships, he sent word

Captain George James, commander of the South Carolina Battalion of Artillery, Company C. In this photograph prior to the war, James is attired in his United States Artillery uniform. *Courtesy of the National Park Service.*

to Anderson in the early morning on Friday, April 12, that he "will open fire of his batteries on Fort Sumter in one hour from this time." Anderson simply responded, "If we never meet in this world again, God grant that we may meet in the next."

Chesnut and Lee left Fort Sumter and retired to Fort Johnson, from which the first shot would be fired. Chesnut and Captain George S. James, commander of the company of Battalion of Artillery, agreed that the beach battery would fire the opening signal shot. James offered the honor of firing the first shot to Roger Pryor, a former congressman from Virginia. Becoming emotionally overwhelmed at the thought, Pryor responded, "I could not fire the first gun of the war." He then got into a boat with three aides and started rowing to Charleston at 4:15 am.

Spectators gathered on piazzas, rooftops and at the Battery in Charleston to watch the pending bombardment. Chesnut ordered James to fire the signal shot at first light. Lieutenant Henry S. Farley, commander of the beach battery, readied the mortar and held the lanyard waiting for the signal. At 4:30 am, James gave the order; Farley pulled the lanyard and fired the signal shot that sailed on a perfect trajectory and exploded over Fort Sumter. By 5:00 am, guns from two James Island batteries, Cummings Point on Morris Island, a battery in Mount Pleasant and Fort Moultrie and the other batteries on Sullivan's Island were firing on Fort Sumter. The *Mercury* reported:

> As may have been anticipated from the notice of the military move-
> ments in our city yesterday, the bombardment of Fort Sumter, so long
> and anxiously expected, has at length become a fact accomplished.
> The restless activity of the night before was gradually worn down,
> the citizens who had thronged the Battery through the night, anx-

In this 1861 *Harper's Weekly* engraving, Anderson's men are attempting to move the gunpowder out of the magazine and away from the fire in Fort Sumter. *Author's Collection.*

> ious and weary, had sought their homes, the Mounted Guard which
> had kept watch and ward over the city, with the first grey streak of
> morning were preparing to retire, when two guns in quick succession
> from Fort Johnson announced the opening of the drama.
>
> Upon that signal, the circle of batteries with which the grim fortress
> of Fort Sumter is beleaguered opened fire. The outline of this great

volcanic crater was illuminated with a line of twinkling lights; the clustering shells illuminated the sky above it; the balls clattering thick as hail upon its sides; our citizens, roused to a forgetfulness of their fatigue through many weary hours, rushed again to the points of observation; and so, at the break of day, amidst the bursting of bombs, the roaring of ordnance, and before thousands of spectators, whose homes, and liberties, and lives were all at stake, was enacted the first great scene in the opening drama of what, it is presumed, will be a most momentous military act.

Sergeant Peter Hart nails the flag to a temporary flagstaff while under fire on April 13, 1861. *Author's Collection.*

Beauregard had instructed the 42 Confederate guns surrounding Fort Sumter to fire in order, in a counterclockwise circle around the harbor, with exactly two minutes in between each shot. However, the excited and inexperienced gunners quickly fell out of order and fired as their guns were ready. The concussion of shells hitting Sumter's walls was felt in Charleston homes more than three miles away. The sound of the bombardment was reported heard as far as forty miles from the harbor.

Anderson did not return fire for several hours. Given his limited manpower, he chose to place his men on the smaller guns in the lowest tier of the fort. Though this did afford protection for his small garrison, the 32- and 42-pound guns could do little damage firing to the Confederate ironclad batteries, sand batteries and the walls of Fort Moultrie, protected by cotton bales. The lower-tier guns would be effective should the Confederate decide to storm the fort.

With the fort under attack, Anderson worked hard to keep his men calm. He took roll call just after 6:00 am and then sent the men to breakfast where they ate the only food left - old salt pork. After breakfast, Anderson divided his troops into groups, one company commanded by Doubleday, the other by Captain Truman Seymour. With a limited amount of cartridges, Anderson ordered that no more than six guns be fired at a time.

One of the greatest threats to Fort Sumter was fire. The interior buildings at the fort and the stairwells connecting the three tiers and ammunition storage were all made of wood. Once the Confederates fired hot-shot, the interior of the fort would incinerate. On the first day of the bombardment, the garrison had to contend with three fires.

Beauregard reported to the Confederate capital, "During the day the fire of my batteries was kept up most spiritedly, the guns and mortars being worked in the coolest manner, preserving the prescribed intervals of firing. Towards the evening it became evident that our fire was very effective."

The Federal ships that had assembled off the coast of Charleston waited in vain for the USS *Powhatan*. Finally, the USS *Harriet Lane* and the USS *Pawnee* moved to the mouth of the harbor. Private Thompson, in Anderson's command at Fort Sumter, wrote,

> *Towards mid-day we could distinctly see a fleet of three war vessels off the bay, and we were certain they were an expedition fitted out to relieve us, and the hopes of speedily getting assistance compensated for the lack of anything in the shape of dinner…We confidently expected the fleet to make some attempt to land supplies and re-enforcements*

during the night, it being dark as pitch and raining, but we were disappointed. Morning dawned and with appetites unappeased and haggard look, although determined and confident, all took their positions for the day's work.

At nightfall, Anderson ordered his guns to cease fire to conserve rounds. His men were served a meal of rancid pork and were assigned to sew more gun cartridges for Saturday. The sentries were posted at Fort Sumter on the lookout for Confederates possibly attempting a landing or, more hopefully, small boats from the Federal fleet to resupply them. Neither event occurred.

The Confederate guns relaxed at night as well. Beauregard had two batteries of mortars fire through the night every fifteen minutes to unsettle the Federal troops at Fort Sumter. Anderson's officers inspected the walls at Fort Sumter and observed that, even though there were many direct hits, the damage was superficial.

During the night, commercial vessels arrived at the mouth of Charleston Harbor, but seeing the mortar fire, did not enter the shipping channel. Sea lightening during the night allowed Confederate sentries to see the number of ships outside the harbor was increasing. They assumed the worst - that these additional ships were Federal warships.

Fox, on the USS *Pawnee* was angry that the *Powhatan* had not arrived, knowing that without her firepower he could not mount a naval attack. He could not send in supplies by small boats, since the *Harriet Lane* had no such boats and the *Pawnee* only one.

The next morning, the Confederate guns began firing again just after daybreak. Like the day before, Anderson had his men stay below to eat their breakfast of pork. With the small number of cartridges available to him, Anderson instructed his men to fire only on Sullivan's Island and fire slowly.

At approximately 9:00 am, a Confederate shell landed on the officers' quarters in Fort Sumter, causing a fire. Everyone from Charleston to the Federal ships on the bar could see the thick, black smoke rising from Fort Sumter. Commander Rowan of the *Pawnee* and Captain Fox felt compelled to help in some way and seized a schooner delivering a load of ice from Boston to Charleston. The plan was to load the civilian ice schooner with supplies and troops to land at Fort Sumter after dark, but it was never implemented.

On Saturday, Pickens wired Governor John Letcher in Virginia, "We can sink the fleet if they attempt to enter the channel. If they land elsewhere we can whip

them…The war is commenced, and we will triumph or perish."

With the fire burning out of control in the fort, Anderson had his men move the three hundred barrels of gunpowder remaining and covering them with wet blankets. With fewer than one hundred barrels of gunpowder moved, the fire was getting too close to the magazine. Anderson ordered the thick metal doors of the magazine closed and the entrance covered with dirt. He ordered that five barrels of gunpowder be retained, but all the others that were removed be thrown over the walls of the fort to the sea. Some of the barrels got hung up on the rocks and did not roll to the water. Finally, a Confederate shell hit them, causing an enormous explosion. Fire also reached a stairwell and implement rooms on the gorge containing several hundred nine-inch grenades, causing them to explode.

During the fight, Fort Sumter's flagstaff was hit seven times during the day. When it finally fell, the Confederates and spectators around the harbor immediately wondered if Anderson was surrendering. The United States flag was promptly nailed to a temporary flagstaff installed on the highest point of the wall.

Colonel Louis T. Wigfall, without orders from Beauregard, took a boat from Cummings Point to Fort Sumter when the storm flag fell. Even though the flag was replaced while he was en route, he continued on to the beleaguered fort. He arrived while the fort was still under fire and was greeted by Foster, Meade and Davis. Wigfall told them, "Your flag is down, you are on fire, and you are not firing your guns. General Beauregard wants you to stop this."

The three officers sent for Anderson. When he arrived, Wigfall said, "You have defended your flag nobly, Sir. You have done all that is possible to do, and General Beauregard wants to stop this fight. On what terms will you evacuate this fort?" Anderson was pleased that Colonel Louis T. Wigfall strategically used the term "evacuate" rather than "surrender." The Federal major indicated that he had already presented his terms to Beauregard days earlier, but that he would evacuate right away rather than wait until April 15. Wigfall left to communicate this to Beauregard and Anderson then ordered the garrison flag down and a white bed sheet was raised over Fort Sumter.

While Wigfall was still in the water, Beauregard sent Stephen Dill Lee, Porcher Miles and Roger Pryor to Fort Sumter, offering assistance with the fire. The three men were surprised that Anderson had already conveyed his agreement to evacuate to Wigfall. They asked Anderson to write down the exact terms agreed to with Wigfall and they would take convey them to Beauregard.

During the bombardment, the Confederate batteries had fired more than 3,300 shots, yet no man at Fort Sumter was killed. The Confederates only suffered two wounded men. Before Lee, Miles and Pryor could depart, two more Beauregard aides arrived. They reported that Beauregard would accept the previous terms discussed on April 11 but the garrison could not salute its flag. Anderson sent the five aides back to town, agreeing to the terms, but he noted that he would appreciate Beauregard's consideration of allowing them to salute the Stars and Stripes on their exit. Beauregard responded back by message:

> *On being informed that you were in distress, caused by a conflagration in Fort Sumter, I immediately dispatched my aides Colonels Miles and Pryor, and Captain Lee, to offer you any assistance in my power to give. Learning a few minutes afterwards that a white flag was waving on your ramparts, I sent two others of my aides, Colonel Allston and Major Jones, to offer you the following terms of evacuation: All proper facilities for the removal of yourself and command, together with company arms and private property, to any point within the United States you may select. Apprised that you desire the privilege of saluting your flag on retiring, I cheerfully concede it, in consideration of the gallantry with which you have defended the place under your charge. The Catawba steamer will be at the landing to-morrow morning at any hour you may designate for the purpose of transporting you whither you may desire.*

Anderson acknowledged the letter and asked that the *Catawba* be at Fort Sumter at 9:00 am.

Charlestonians responded with great celebrations, bonfires and fireworks on hearing the news of the surrender. One woman exclaimed, "Wonderful, miraculous, unheard of in history, a bloodless victory." Charlestonian Henry William Ravenel pondered, "The first act in the drama is over! Will it end thus, or is it only the opening of a bloody tragedy?"

On Sunday morning, Confederate Commander Henry J. Hartstene, C.S. Navy arrived at Fort Sumter before dawn informing them that the steamer *Isabel* would pick them up and transport them to the Federal ships at the bar. In Charleston, Pickens declared Sunday to be "A Day of National Fasting, Thanksgiving, and Prayer." Many Charlestonians booked passage on boats to the harbor to watch the retiring of the United States flag and the raising of the South Carolina and Confederate flags.

Anderson presented the keys to Fort Sumter to Beauregard's aide, Captain Sam Ferguson, who was accompanied by a company of the Palmetto Guard. At 2:30 pm, Anderson and his men assembled on the parade ground as the United States flag was raised for the last time. While Fort Sumter's guns were firing their salute, one of the guns discharged prematurely, killing Private Daniel Hough and wounding the other members of the gun crew. Private Edward Gallway and Private George Fielding were transported to the hospital in Charleston, but Gallway died later that night. Three other wounded men were put aboard the *Isabel* and Hough was buried on the parade ground in the fort.

It was almost 4:30 pm when the garrison finally marched out of the fort to the tune of "Yankee Doodle," followed by "Hail to the Chief." With the long delay, the *Isabel* was now grounded on a shoal due to low tide and Anderson and his men had to stay onboard overnight, listening to the speeches of the Confederates in their fort.

That night, Pickens, ecstatic with the victory, gave a speech from the balcony of the Charleston Hotel:

> *We have defeated their twenty millions. We have humbled the flag of the United States before the Palmetto and Confederate, and so long as I have the honor to preside as your chief magistrate, so help me God, there is no power on earth shall ever lower from that fortress those flags, unless they be lowered and trailed in a sea of blood. I can here say to you it is the first time in the history of this country that the stars and stripes have been humbled. That flag has never before been lowered before any nation on this earth. But today it has been humbled and humbled before the glorious little State of South Carolina.*

The next morning, the tide released the *Isabel* from the shoal and the Federal troops were transferred to the USS *Baltic*, where Anderson wrote his final report to Secretary of War Cameron:

> *Having defended Fort Sumter for thirty-four hours, until the quarters were entirely burned, the main gates destroyed by fire, the gorge walls seriously impaired, the magazine surrounded by flames, and its door closed from the effects of the heat, four barrels and three cartridges of powder only being available, and no provisions remaining but pork, I accepted the terms of General Beauregard (being the same offered by him on the 11th instant, prior to the commencement of hostilities) and marched out of the Fort on Sunday afternoon, the 14th instant, with colors flying and drums beating, bringing away company and private property, and saluting my flag with fifty guns.*
> *Robert Anderson, Major, First Artillery*

Big Red

"Big Red" *Courtesy of the State Historical Society of Iowa.*

The flag was donated to an Iowa museum in 1919 by Union veteran Private John Baker. Ignored for decades, "Big Red" was discovered in storage at the State Historical Society of Iowa and is now on loan to The Citadel.

After extensive research, it is believed that "Big Red" was in the possession of Captain James Furman Culpepper, Citadel class of 1854, who commanded Company C of the Palmetto Artillery. Culpepper's unit was posted at Fort Blakeley, Alabama, where they were attacked and captured by Union troops on April 9, 1865. First Lieutenant Joshua L. Moses, Citadel class of 1860, and other soldiers with connections to the Citadel were also at Fort Blakeley.

The 20th Iowa Volunteer Infantry was involved in the capture of Fort Blakeley. After capture, the possessions of the Confederate troops were confiscated. Union Private Willard Baker, a member of Company C of the 20th Iowa, procured the flag on or about April 14, 1865.

A replica of "Big Red" was adopted as the spirit flag for the Citadel Corps of Cadets in 1992. The replica featured a white palmetto with a white outward facing crescent on a red field. Interestingly, when the real flag was discovered, the Citadel found that it featured an inward facing crescent. In 2009, the Citadel's Board of Visitors adopted the original flag design as the academy's official spirit flag.

In January 1861, 50 student cadets from The Citadel, under the command of superintendent Major Peter F. Stevens, were deployed to Morris Island where they erected Fort Morris. While on the island, they were presented with a red palmetto flag by the women of the Vincent family, the family that owned most of Morris Island at the time. The flag was made by Hugh Vincent. The flag was described in the *Charleston Daily Courier* as a "white palmetto tree on a blood red field." This flag flew over Fort Morris when the cadets forced the *Star of the West* to turn back on January 9, unable to reinforce and re-supply Fort Sumter. Despite being lost during the war, this flag, affectionately known as "Big Red," became infamous in Citadel lore.

In November 2009, NASA astronaut Marine Lt. Colonel Randy Bresnik, Citadel Class of 1989, took a replica of "Big Red" with him to the International Space Station. Bresnik presented his flag to the Citadel on March 19, 2010. That same day, each of the five battalions of the Corps of Cadets carried replicas of the original "Big Red" in their dress parade for the first time.

Pierre Gustave Toutant Beauregard

Pierre Gustave Toutant Beauregard was born on May 28, 1818, at Contreras, a sugar-cane plantation in St. Bernard Parish, Louisiana. He attended school in New Orleans and a French school in New York, where he learned to speak English.

Beauregard enrolled at West Point where his favorite professor was Robert Anderson, his artillery instructor. The two often dined together in the evening and developed a close friendship. Beauregard graduated second in his class in 1838, and displayed an exceptional talent as an engineer.

Beauregard was commissioned as a 2nd lieutenant in the United States Army. During the Mexican War, he served as General Winfield Scott's military engineer. He participated in the Battles of Contreras, Churubusco and Chapultepec, earning the rank of brevet major by the war's end. He distinguished himself on reconnaissance missions and with his excellent strategic plans. He returned to New Orleans in 1848, and, for the next 12 years, served as chief engineer for the "Mississippi and Lake Defenses in Louisiana."

With the help of his brother-in-law, Beauregard was appointed superintendent of the United States Military Academy at West Point. Upon acceptance, he made it clear to the secretary of war that if Louisiana seceded from the Union, he would find it necessary to resign his post in support of his native state. Beauregard reported to West Point on January 23, 1861. Louisiana seceded on January 26 and his appointment was revoked the next day.

Beauregard received the first appointment to general made by the newly elected Confederate President Jefferson Davis on March 1, 1861. Brigadier General Beauregard was sent to Charleston to assume command of all Confederate forces. Unable to convince his former mentor to evacuate his garrison and with the Federal warships arriving at the mouth of Charleston Harbor on the night of April 11, Beauregard ordered the bombardment of Fort Sumter on the morning of April 12, 1861.

Brigadier General P. G. T. Beauregard. *Courtesy of the National Archives.*

He was transferred to Virginia, and on July 21, 1861, defeated Union Brigadier General Irvin McDowell, one of his West Point classmates, at the First Battle of Bull Run. Two days later, President Davis promoted Beauregard to the rank of full general.

After a fallout with Davis, Beauregard was transferred to Tennessee where he was second in command to General Albert Sidney Johnston for the Battle of Shiloh (Tennessee). After Johnston's death at Shiloh, Beauregard commanded the Confederate forces at the Battle of Corinth (Mississippi). In 1863, he was sent back to Charleston, replacing John C. Pemberton as commander, and prevented the capture of Charleston. In 1864, he assisted Robert E. Lee with the defense of Richmond. Davis then appointed Beauregard as commander of Confederate forces in the West. With few assets in troops and supplies, he had no way to slow the advances of Union General William T. Sherman. On April 26, 1865, Beauregard and General Joe Johnston surrendered to Sherman near Durham, North Carolina.

A Courier & Ives engraving of the 1863 ironclad attack on Fort Sumter. *Courtesy of the Library of Congress.*

Attack of the Ironclads

After the withdrawal of the Union troops on April 14, 1861, a reporter for the Charleston *Mercury* reported on the conditions inside Fort Sumter:

> *Every point and every object in the interior of the fort, to which the eye was turned, except the outer walls and casemates, which are still strong, bore the impress of ruin…The walls of the internal structure– roofless, bare, bleak and perforated by shot and shell–hung in fragments, and seemed in instant readiness to totter down. Near the centre of the parade ground was the hurried grave of the one who had fallen from the recent casualty…And so it was that the garrison, compelled to yield the fortress, had at least the satisfaction of leaving it in a condition calculated to inspire the least possible pleasure to its captors.*

The honor to occupy Fort Sumter the first night of Confederate control was given to the Palmetto Guard and Company B , South Carolina Battalion of Artillery. The Palmetto Guard, with the help of the Charleston Fire Department, worked to extinguish the fires still burning in the fort. The fire department brought out their new "experimental" steam pumper for use at Fort Sumter. Though many in Charleston were leery of this new steam engine contraption, it performed admirably at the fort. Work began immediately on Fort Sumter to rebuild and alter the interior of the fort.

On April 19, 1861, Lincoln issued a proclamation calling for the blockade of all Southern ports. On May 11, the USS *Niagara* was the first ship to arrive at the mouth of Charleston Harbor. She was later joined by other ships, but the Charleston blockade was largely ineffective. By August, Union General Thomas W. Sherman was ordered by the secretary of war to start recruiting an army in the New England states for an attack on the Southern coast.

Though Beauregard and Pickens disagreed on the locations and defensive

The interior of Fort Sumter after occupation by Confederate troops on April 14, 1861, published in *Frank Leslie's Illustrated News. Author's Collection.*

strategy to protect Port Royal, Beaufort and Hilton Head, the governor ordered two forts to be erected at the entrance to the Port Royal Harbor, Fort Walker on Hilton Head and Fort Beauregard at Bay Point. Beauregard was soon called to Virginia and Major Francis D. Lee was tasked with building the two new forts.

Lincoln favored an expedition against Port Royal to establish a Union base of operations on the southern coast for an eventual attack on Charleston and a great force was organized for the task. Fifteen men-of-war with a total of

148 guns were assembled under the command of Flag Officer Samuel F. Du Pont. The Union army assembled 12,653 troops and 36 transports under the command of Brigadier General Thomas W. Sherman. The first of the Federal ships left New York Harbor to assemble at Hampton Roads, Virginia.

The Confederacy organized the Department of South Carolina, Georgia and East Florida and tapped Robert E. Lee as commander. Lee arrived in Charleston

Brigadier General Thomas Sherman. *Courtesy of the Library of Congress.*

by train on November 6. Hearing of a large Federal fleet assembling off the coast of Port Royal, he traveled south the next morning.

As Lee was en route, the Federal fleet attacked the two forts, causing the abandonment of both Forts Walker and Beauregard. Total casualties on both sides were less than 100, but the Battle of Port Royal was the first important Union victory of the war. With the fall of Port Royal and the subsequent capture of Beaufort and St. Helena Sound, Lincoln had what he wanted – a base of operations for the assault on Charleston.

The Union needed to find an effective method to blockade the Southern ports without maintaining a large fleet along the entire coastline. The decision was made to block the shipping channels with sunken schooners, thinking this would prevent deep-draft ships from safely passing to and from the harbors.

On November 20, 1861, 25 schooners, outfitted with removable plugs in the hull, left New Bedford, Massachusetts for Charleston and Savannah. Fifteen of the schooners arrived at the mouth of Charleston Harbor on December 19. Once they were positioned properly, the plugs were removed, sinking the ships and blocking the main shipping channel. The ships in this sunken blockade were referred to as the "stone fleet."

Lee reacted with disgust in a telegram to the Confederate secretary of war, stating:

> *This achievement, so unworthy of any nation, is the abortive expression of malice and revenge of a people which it wishes to perpetuate by rendering more memorable a day hateful in their calendar. It is also indicative of their despair of ever capturing a city they design to ruin. . .*

An 1861 engraving of Samuel F. Du Pont, published in *Harper's Weekly. Author's Collection.*

The Battle of Port Royal. *Author's Collection.*

Even though an additional 14 ships were also scuttled in the Maffitt's Channel off Sullivan's Island in January, high tides, strong winds and swift currents destroyed the "stone fleet," leaving the harbor open. On March 2, 1862, Lee was recalled to Richmond and Major General John C. Pemberton was placed in command in Charleston.

Union General Sherman asked his chief engineer, Captain Quincy A. Gillmore, to formulate options for the capture of Charleston. After study and consideration, Gillmore proposed two options. The first plan called for amphibious landings on Sullivan's and Morris Islands to lay siege on Fort Sumter. Once the threat of Fort Sumter was eliminated, the Union fleet could sail into the inner harbor and capture the city. The second was to capture James Island. Placing Union siege batteries on the island's northern shore would place the harbor forts in a weak position and threaten Charleston.

By spring 1862, the decision was made to open a joint army-navy operation on James Island by moving up the Stono River. Earlier Confederate General

Pemberton removed the battery at Coles Island near the mouth of the Stono River, thus allowing Union gunboats to enter the river and reach the south side of James Island unimpeded. The Union plan was to land on James Island and take Fort Johnson. This would isolate Forts Sumter and Moultrie, effectively giving the Union command control of the inner harbor.

By mid-May, Union gunboats were spotted at the mouth of the Stono River. By the end of May, the Union navy had six gunboats in place. Five other gunboats and two barges served as troop transports. On June 2, Major General David Hunter, commanding 6,600 troops, traveled from Port Royal to the Stono River where they landed on James Island at Grimball Plantation. Over the next several days, additional Union troops arrived by transport and by crossing Johns Island to reach the Stono River.

After three minor skirmishes with Confederate troops, Hunter was stalled with his troops on the southwestern side of James Island and Sol Legare Island. Hunter returned to Port Royal and left General Henry Benham in command, but

Brigadier General Henry Benham. *Courtesy of the Library of Congress.*

with instructions not to advance and attack. After being shelled by Confederate artillery, Benham decided to advance, if only to capture the Confederate guns harassing him.

Before dawn on June 16, Benham advanced on the "Tower Battery", a Confederate position at Secessionville and, perhaps, the strongest point of the Confederate defenses on James Island. Though he caught the Confederate battery by surprise, Benham was soundly defeated and he ordered a retreat by 9:45 am.

Union Colonel Daniel Leasure with the 100th Pennsylvania Infantry would later write:

I advanced with the left flank of the Highlanders, cheering them to the charge, till when within about one hundred yards of the works three immense guns bellowed out a perfect cloud of grape, canister, old chains, empty porter bottles, nails and even brickets, and just cut the regiment in two . . . Panic and disaster were imminent every minute . . .

Union forces suffered 700 casualties, while the Confederates had only 150. Hunter relieved Benham of command and sent him to Hilton Head, where he was arrested for disobedience of orders. The defeat convinced Hunter to remove his troops from James Island on July 8.

By the fall of 1862, the navy was pressuring Du Pont to attack Charleston with his ironclad fleet. The Union blockade of Charleston, though ineffective, was still in place. Du Pont had six steamships and two sailing ships deployed in an arc 13 miles long. He was not confident with this strategy and expressed to his wife by letter that the ships would "be firing into each other at the first alarm."

On September 24, 1862, Beauregard returned to Charleston where, once again, he assumed command. He would use the next six months to work on new shorter defensive lines and increasing the armament in the harbor forts. He

Union troops are advancing on the Tower Battery during the Battle of Secessionville in this 1862 engraving published in *Frank Leslie's Illustrated News. Author's Collection.*

also deployed two ironclads, harbor obstructions, torpedoes and fire rafts in his strategy for the defense of Charleston. Beauregard believed the next attempt to take Charleston would be a naval attack.

In the spring of 1863, South Carolina appropriated $50,000 for the construction of six steam rams armed with spar torpedoes on the front. Fixed torpedoes were placed in the Ashley River, protecting the south side of Charleston. A large torpedo was placed in the shipping channel, one mile from Fort Sumter. This torpedo, 18 feet long and three feet in diameter, was made from a boiler and contained 3,000 pounds of powder,

Beauregard designed three interlocking circles of fire on any ship entering the harbor. Fort Sumter was the center of the first line which included Batteries Gregg and Wagner on Morris Island to the south and Fort Moultrie, Fort Beauregard, Batteries Bee, Marion, Marshall and four small batteries, all on Sullivan's Island. The second circle included Fort Johnson and Batteries Cheves, Wampler and Glover on James Island; Fort Ripley and Castle Pinckney in the harbor; a battery on Hog Island and two batteries on Mount Pleasant. The final circle included batteries in Charleston and others on the banks of the Ashley and Cooper Rivers. Range buoys were placed throughout the harbor to assist the Confederate gunners with the accuracy of their fire.

Union Brigadier General Truman Seymour made a reconnaissance of the outer harbor at Charleston. He recommended to General Hunter troops be deployed to Morris Island, capture Battery Wagner and use breeching batteries on Morris Island and the Union fleet to capture Fort Sumter. Hunter made Seymour his chief-of-staff and chief-of-artillery but did not act on his recommendation.

In February 1863, the Union command sent 10,000 troops, commanded by Major General John G.

A "powder monkey" aboard a Union ship off the coast of Charleston blockading the harbor. *Courtesy of the Library of Congress.*

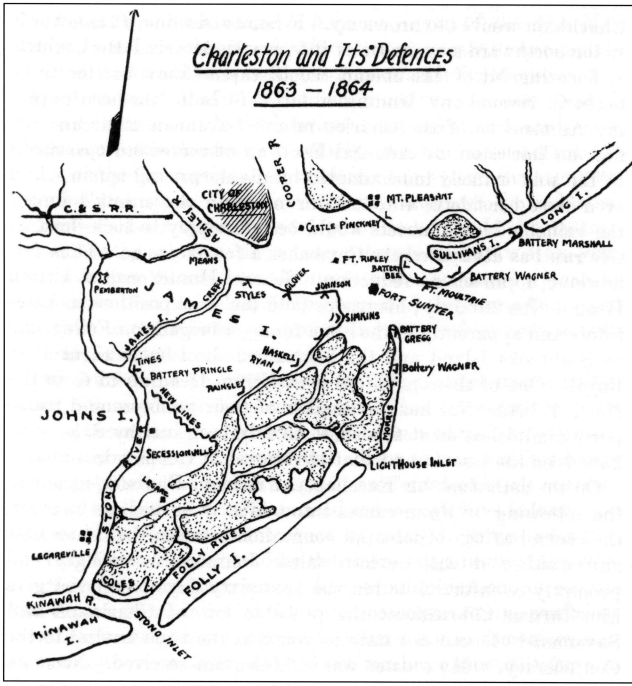

Charleston and Its Defences
1863 – 1864

C. & S. R. R.

CITY OF CHARLESTON

COOPER R.

ASHLEY R.

MT. PLEASANT

CASTLE PINCKNEY

LONG I.

FT. RIPLEY
Battery BEE

SULLIVANS I.

BATTERY MARSHALL

MEANS

PEMBERTON

JAMES I.

GLOVER

STYLES

JOHNSON

FORT SUMTER

FT. MOULTRIE

BATTERY WAGNER

SIMKINS

BATTERY GREGG

TINES

HASKELL

RYAN

BATTERY PRINGLE

RAINSLEY

JOHNS I.

NEW LINES

SECESSIONVILLE

LEGARE B

LIGHT HOUSE INLET

MORRIS

Battery WAGNER

LEGAREVILLE

STONO RIVER

COLES

KINAWAH R.

KINAWAH I.

FOLLY RIVER

FOLLY I.

STONO INLET

A map of Charleston and its defenses, 1863-1864. *Courtesy of Willis J. Keith.*

Foster, to Hilton Head for operations against Charleston. Foster favored Gillmore's plan of operations against Morris and Sullivan's Islands, setting up a conflict between Hunter and Foster.

In assessing a naval attack on Charleston, Du Pont referred to the harbor as "a good deal like a porcupine's hide and quills turned outside in and served up at one end." He relied on Confederate deserters and escaped slaves for reconnaissance on the Confederate defenses. Despite this intelligence, he did not fully appreciate the firepower assembled in Charleston Harbor nor the challenge of moving through the swift channel.

Du Pont continued to be pressured by Assistant Secretary of the Navy Gustavus Fox to move on Charleston. Du Pont was concerned about the ability of the ironclad ships to handle the shot that would be fired on them. He wrote Secretary of the Navy Gideon Welles stating that Fox "overrates the monitors as much as he underrates the defenses" of Charleston. Lincoln met with his naval and army commanders to discuss the progress of the war. Foster, once again, pitched his proposal to capture Charleston by, first, taking Morris Island. Lincoln expressed his concern that approaching by Morris Island could result in a protracted siege. Like Welles and Fox, the president favored a naval attack.

Fox was sent to Port Royal to meet with Du Pont and suggested, "Go in and demand a surrender of the forts or the alternative of destruction to their city." By March 1863, Du Pont had assembled seven monitors, the USS *Keokuk* and the USS *New Ironsides*, totaling 32 guns. Du Pont was also instructed to build rafts on the bow of the monitors to clear any obstructions or torpedoes they might encounter in Charleston Harbor. Du Pont expressed, "I have no more idea that we can use them than we can fly."

The Union plan was for the *Keokuk* to move in and buoy the channel. The *Weehawken*, rigged with a torpedo raft, would lead the attack, followed by the *Passaic, Montauk, Patapsco, New Ironsides, Catskill, Nantucket, Nahant* and *Keokuk*. Their orders were to steam up the main channel, ignore the batteries on Morris Island and attack the northwest face of Fort Sumter.

By April 5, Du Pont's ironclads began to assemble outside the Charleston Harbor shipping channel. On the morning of April 7, Confederate Colonel Alfred Rhett telegrammed the city announcing, "The turrets are coming," referring to the pillbox turrets on top of the monitors. Charlestonians assembled in great numbers at the Battery and on the rooftops and steeples to watch the naval attack.

The Union ships began moving at noon, but the advance stalled as the *Weehawken* was having trouble with the raft on its bow. By 2:30 pm, the Confederate garrison at Fort Sumter was called to their guns. The fort's band played as the Palmetto flag, the garrison flag and the South Carolina 1st Artillery flag were raised over the fort. Fort Sumter fired a 13-gun salute and prepared to face the oncoming ships.

When the *Weehawken* came within range, Fort Moultrie opened fire, hitting the ship's turret and the side of the ironclad at the waterline. The *Passaic* fired first on the bellowing guns at Fort Moultrie. The *New Ironsides*, with her flat bottom, was having trouble in the channel and she stopped.

As the *Weehawken* passed a range buoy, all the guns at Fort Sumter and on Sullivan's and Morris

Officers on the deck of the monitor USS *Catskill. Courtesy of the Library of Congress.*

Charlestonians gather on The Battery to watch the ironclad attack on Fort Sumter. Sketched by Frank Vizetelly and published in the *Illustrated London News*. *Author's Collection*

The *Weehawken* leading the attack, published in *Frank Leslie's Illustrated News. Author's Collection.*

Islands opened fire. In the ensuing confusion, the *Catskill* and *Nantucket* collided with *New Ironsides*, now sitting still. Water spray created by the many shots hitting and landing near the *Weehawken*, left the ship's pilot and gunners blind. The *Weehawken* was under intense fire for 40 minutes and the effective shots destroyed much of her armor and pierced her deck.

The *Passaic*, commanded by Percival Drayton, a native South Carolinian, managed to fire 13 shots but was hit 34 times by Confederate fire. One shot struck the turret and ricocheted to hit the pilothouse. The intense fire and damage forced the *Passaic* to retire to repair damage.

The slow, cumbersome monitors were no match for all the Confederate guns.

The monitors attack Fort Sumter in this 1863 *Harper's Weekly* engraving. *Author's Collection.*

ironclads suffered enough damage to disable the ships. One officer observed, the *Keokuk* was "riddled like a colander." The ship retired 1,400 yards south of Morris Island and sank the next day.

On the next morning, Du Pont met with his senior officers aboard his flagship, the *New Ironsides*. All agreed that the attack should not continue, with Du Pont stating he did not want to turn "failure into disaster." Du Pont wrote in his report to Washington, "I attempted to take the bull by the horns, but he was too much for us. These monitors are miserable failures where forts are concerned." In a letter to his wife written aboard ship, Du Pont confided, "We have failed as I felt sure we would."

While some of the Union guns left craters in Fort Sumter's walls 2 ½ feet deep, the damage to the fort was minimal. Working at night to avoid being seen by the Union ships stationed offshore, the Confederates salvaged the guns from the *Keokuk*. A workforce of 500 slaves were put to work on Fort Sumter filling casemates with sand, sandbagging the gorge wall and constructing bombproof shelters. While some of Fort Sumter's guns were removed, many of the heaviest guns were moved to the barbette, on top of the wall, to give them the widest angles of fire possible on attacking ships.

The sinking of the *Keokuk*, published in *Harper's Weekly. Author's Collection*.

Even after the *Catskill, Nantucket, Nahant* and *Keokuk* navigated around the *New Ironsides*, they could not fire nearly as many rounds as they were receiving. All of the ironclads were suffering damage that, in many cases, disabled the ship or jammed their turret. The *Keokuk* was having trouble in the swift current. She was hit 90 times and her light armor could not adequately protect the ship. Nineteen of those shots either pierced the hull or hit below the waterline.

In the 2 ½ hour battle, the Union ironclads only managed to fire 154 rounds and only 34 of them hit their target. The many Confederate batteries and Fort Sumter fired 2,209 rounds with 520 of them hitting Union ships. Five of the

Though the attacking ironclads withdrew, Union troops remained in position on Folly and Seabrook Islands. Since the bold naval attack did not work, the Union command began debating options for the siege of Charleston. On July 6, 1863, command of the South Atlantic Blockading Squadron was transferred from Du Pont to Rear Admiral John A. Dahlgren.

Alfred Moore Rhett

Alfred Moore Rhett was the son of Robert Barnwell Rhett, the influential secessionist politician. Raised in a wealthy family, his father sought the best education for Alfred and he was sent to Harvard, where he graduated in 1851.

After South Carolina seceded from the Union, Rhett volunteered for service to the state by joining the South Carolina Battalion of Artillery. He was a 1st Lieutenant stationed at Fort Moultrie.

While posting at Forts Moultrie and Sumter, Rhett grew to dislike a fellow officer, W. Ransom Calhoun, a nephew of South Carolina's most notable statesman – John C. Calhoun. During the April 1861 bombardment on Fort Sumter, Captain Calhoun gave orders directly to Rhett's company, rather than through Rhett, ignoring the proper chain of command. He also cursed and dressed down Rhett in front of his men. Rhett retaliated by repeatedly publicly ridiculing Calhoun. Calhoun was promoted to colonel over Rhett, then a major. After several months of this tension, Calhoun challenged Rhett to a duel.

On September 22, 1862, Calhoun and Rhett, accompanied by their seconds and surgeons, traveled to Charleston to settle their differences. Facing each other at 10 paces, both men fired pistols. Calhoun was hit by Rhett's shot. He staggered and fell into the arms of his second. He was taken to the residence of Mitchell King in Charleston where he died within the hour. Despite a protest by the Confederate secretary of war, General Beauregard approved Rhett's promotion

Colonel Alfred Rhett, Confederate commander of Fort Sumter, 1862-1863. *Courtesy of Willis J. Keith.*

to colonel and was given command of Calhoun's unit at Fort Sumter.

Rhett commanded the garrison at Fort Sumter from April to September 1863. During his tenure as commander he faced Du Pont's monitor attack in April and the first great bombardment of Fort Sumter in the summer. In September, Beauregard transferred Rhett from Fort Sumter to command the inner harbor fortifications. In the summer of 1864, Rhett was one of two men recommended to command the First Military District in South Carolina; however the command was given to Major General Robert Ransom. Rhett remained in Charleston until the evacuation of the city in February 1865.

With other South Carolina troops, Rhett, now commanding a brigade, reinforced Joe Johnston's army in North Carolina. He was captured by Union Captain Theo Northrop at the Battle of Averasboro (North Carolina) on March 16, 1865. He was sent to a prison in New York in April with 900 other Confederate prisoners captured by Sherman's troops at Bentonville, Goldsboro and Columbia. The notoriety of the Rhett family name and his reputation for serving as commander at Fort Sumter made Colonel Rhett's arrival in New York big news as it was covered by the New York Times. Rhett survived a short stay in prison and, after his parole, returned to Charleston.

After the war, Rhett served as chief constable for South Carolina. While serving in this position, he wrote a 41-page defense of dueling.

John Adolphus Bernard Dahlgren

John Dahlgren was born in Philadelphia on November 13, 1809, the son of Swedish Consul Bernhard Ulrik Dahlgren. Dahlgren joined the United States Navy in 1826 as a midshipman.

By 1847, he was an ordnance officer, an area in which he possessed a natural talent. Dahlgren established the Navy's Ordnance Department and over the next 15 years he invented a number of guns for naval service, including bronze boat guns, heavy smoothbore shell guns, and rifled ordnance. He also authored a number of books, including *The System of Boat Armaments in the United States Navy*, *Shells and Shell Guns*, and *Naval Percussion Locks and Primers*. His work at the Washington Navy Yard was the first weapons research and development program in the navy, earning him the deserved reference as "the father of American naval ordnance."

In the Navy's foundry in Washington, Dahlgren's first project was the "Boat Howitzer," which could be used on ship and in landings on shore. He later developed a cast iron muzzle loading cannon that came to be known as the "Dahlgren gun," favored for its lightness, range and accuracy. By 1856, the Dahlgren gun was the standard armament for the United States Navy.

In 1861, Dahlgren's commanding officer at the Washington Navy Yard resigned to join the Confederate Navy. President Lincoln persuaded Congress to pass an act to allow Commander Dahlgren to accept command of the Navy Yard, though standing law required the position to be filled by a captain or higher rank. In July 1862, Dahlgren was promoted to captain and made chief of the Bureau of Ordnance. In February 1863, he was promoted to rear admiral.

After Samuel Du Pont's monitor attack on Fort Sumter failed in April 1863, Dahlgren was promoted, with Lincoln's support, to command of the South Atlantic Blockading Squadron in July 1863. He spent two long frustrating years on the siege of Charleston. Just as the British experienced in 1776, Dahlgren found that Charleston could not be taken by a naval attack. He never could solve the challenge of the city's underwater mines and torpedoes and Fort Sumter was his nemesis.

After the war, Dahlgren served a stint as commander at the South Pacific Squadron. In 1869, he, once again, accepted command of the Washington Navy Yard, a position he held until his death in July 1870.

Rear Admiral Dahlgren on the USS *Pawnee*, standing next to a Dahlgren gun. *Courtesy of the Library of Congress.*

Dahlgren's son, Colonel Ulric Dahlgren was killed in 1864 while leading a cavalry raid on Richmond to assassinate Jefferson Davis and the Confederate cabinet.

Interestingly, Dahlgren's younger brother, Charles G. Dahlgren was an ardent supporter of slavery and served with the Bank of the United States in Natchez, Mississippi prior to the war. After Mississippi seceded from the Union, Charles raised two regiments of state militia with his own money to form the 3rd Brigade, Army of Mississippi. He vehemently objected when his brigade was transferred from state service to the Provisional Army of the Confederate States and lost his command.

Monitors

The Civil War was a time of great military and technological innovation. The Siege of Charleston bore witness to the development of new types of mines and a new class of steam-powered, torpedo boats – the Davids. Charleston Harbor was also the site of the first submarine to sink an enemy warship when the *H. L. Hunley* attacked the USS *Housatonic* on February 17, 1864.

John Ericsson, a Swedish-born inventor and mechanical engineer, changed the face of the United States Navy with his invention of the *Monitor* class of ironclad war ships. As early as 1820, Ericsson was tinkering with steam engines and twin-propeller propulsion. The first ship designed and engineered by Ericsson for the

In 1861, after Virginia seceded from the Union, the United States Navy decided to destroy the Gosport Shipyard in Portsmouth, Virginia, rather than let it fall under the control of the Confederates. They set fire to the USS *Merrimack*, but she sank before the fire consumed the entire ship. The Confederates raised the hull of the ship and used it to build the CSS *Virginia*, a steam-powered ironclad warship. In response to this development, in August 1861, Congress authorized the development of armored ships for the Navy.

Cornelius Bushnell, a railroad executive and shipbuilder, convinced Ericsson to work with the Navy to build a new class of armored ships. The ironclad was described as a "cheesebox on a raft." One hundred days after the ship was laid down, the Navy launched the USS *Monitor* on March 6, 1862.

The initial design called for the installation of a large revolving gun turret, housing two 11-inch Dahlgren guns. The cylindrical turret was 20 feet in diameter, nine feet high and covered with eight layers on one-inch iron. The "cheesebox" rotated on a spindle, powered by a steam engine. The pilot house was forward of the turret on the main deck. This proved to be a flaw as it prohibited the guns from firing forward.

Other than the turret, the pilot house and a smokestack, the bulk of the ship was below the waterline. This was designed intending to protect the hull from cannon fire. The crew for the *Monitor* included 59 officers and men.

Only three days after her launch, the *Monitor* was sent to Hampton Roads, Virginia, where she faced the Confederate ironclad CSS *Virginia*. Though the Battle of Hampton Roads was a draw, the *Monitor* became the prototype for a new ironclad warship and the United States Navy began construction of 10 more monitors. These additional monitors were larger than the original *Monitor* and placed the pilot house atop the gun turret, giving the ship a wider field of

Diagram of a monitor, published in The Illustrated London News, 1862. *Author's Collection.*

Navy was the USS *Princeton*, the first screw steam warship, launched in 1843. In 1854, Ericsson presented Napoleon III with a proposal for ironclad battleships with a "dome-shaped" gun tower. The French emperor was impressed with the design but did not commission any to be built.

fire. These monitors were referred to as *Passaic* class monitors, named for the USS *Passaic*, the first of the 10 constructed. Other monitors in this class were the *Montauk, Nahant, Patapsco, Weehawken, Sangamon, Catskill, Nantucket, Lehigh* and *Comanche*, seven of which were involved in the April 7, 1863 attack on Fort Sumter. Later models of monitors featured two or three turrets.

Union Secretary of the Navy Gideon Welles felt that the monitors, combined with other ironclad warships, held great promise for the Navy in the war. Flag Officer Samuel Du Pont, commander of the South Atlantic Blockading Squadron, was less certain. Du Pont recognized the defensive capabilities of the monitors but he felt their limited offensive firepower was a concern.

He decided to test the monitors with an attack on Fort McAlister, a small three-gun earthwork battery in Georgia, on March 3, 1863. The *Patapsco, Passaic* and *Nahant* were sent by Du Pont under the command of Percival Drayton to test the effectiveness of their fire on a shore battery. After an eight-hour bombardment, Fort McAlister was still operational and capable of returning fire.

Officers on the deck and turret of the monitor USS Catskill. *Courtesy of the Library of Congress.*

The experience at Fort McAlister did little to bolster the confidence of Du Pont. He felt the monitors were ineffective against an earthworks battery. Additionally, he felt their rate of fire would be a concern when facing a masonry fort.

Welles and Assistant Secretary of the Navy Gustavus Fox were convinced that a monitor attack on Charleston would not only result in the capture of the secessionist city, but would be a prestigious victory for the Navy. As Du Pont expressed his doubts about the effectiveness of the monitors, Welles felt that Du Pont "shrinks from responsibility, dreads the conflict he has sought, yet is unwilling that any other should undertake it, is afraid the reputation of Du Pont will suffer."

Even Ericsson, the monitors' designer, was not optimistic about an ironclad attack on Charleston. In writing the Navy, he expressed, "Your confidence in the great naval attack astounds me – you have not turrets enough . . . you have not guns enough." In response, Welles and Fox increased the number of monitors for the attack, and sent the Keokuk, a twin-tower experimental ironclad, and the New Ironsides, the strongest ship in the Navy, heavily armed with 16 guns, to participate in the battle.

Du Pont's premonition was correct. The monitors' poor maneuverability and slow speed proved problematic. Most of all, their slow rate of fire resulted in only 154 rounds fired, compared to the Confederates' return fire totaling 2,209 rounds.

Statue in Battery Park, New York, honoring John Ericsson, designer for the monitors. *Courtesy of the Library of Congress.*

In his report to Washington, Du Pont asserted, "I attempted to take the bull by the horns, but he was too much for us. These monitors are miserable failures where forts are concerned."

Painting by Seth Eastman of Fort Sumter after the Union bombardment. *Courtesy of the Collection of the US House of Representatives.*

The Defense of Sumter

By the summer of 1863, Beauregard assumed that the Union army would move from Folly Island to Morris Island and, from there, attempt to capture Fort Sumter. He stated confidently, "They will find that to be a piece of folly."

Before Pemberton was removed from command in Charleston he ordered the erection of a battery across the narrowest point on Morris Island. The battery, 1,300 yards from Cummings Point, was first called the "Neck Battery," but later named Battery Wagner in honor of Lt. Colonel Thomas Wagner of the 1st Regiment, South Carolina Artillery who was killed at Fort Moultrie. Work was complete on Battery Wagner by June 1863.

On June 12, 1863, Quincy A. Gillmore, now a Brigadier General, was given command of the Department of the South for the Union army. He revived his old plan for the capture of Charleston written when he was chief engineer for General Sherman. Gillmore planned to capture the southern end of Morris Island, eliminate Battery Wagner, reduce Fort Sumter to rubble, making it possible for the Union navy to reach the inner harbor of Charleston and force the city's surrender.

In setting his sights on Fort Sumter over an approach to Charleston through James Island, Gillmore wrote General Henry W. Halleck, Lincoln's General-in-Chief, "The answer is simple. The enemy had more troops available for the defense of Charleston than we had for the attack." Gillmore, however, was wrong. He had 11,500 troops assembled on Folly and Seabrook Islands ready to assault Charleston while Beauregard only had 5,841 troops to defend the region.

On July 10, 1863, 47 guns on Little Folly opened fire on the Confederate troops stationed on the southern end of Morris Island. Admiral Dahlgren joined the attack with the *Catskill, Nahant, Montauk* and the *Weehawken*. After three hours of continuous bombardment, 2,000 Union troops crossed Lighthouse Inlet

to Morris Island. Dahlgren's monitors began to take on fire as they neared the Confederate stronghold, Battery Wagner. The Confederate forces fell back to Battery Wagner and the Union army was able to secure the southern end of Morris Island. Believing that James Island was the key to Charleston, Beauregard chose not to take Confederate troops from the island to reinforce Morris Island.

The next day, Gillmore ordered an attack on Battery Wagner, thinking he could quickly overwhelm the sand fort. Four companies of the 7th Connecticut, supported by the 76th Pennsylvania and the 9th Maine, made the assault. The Union troops suffered 339 casualties in a fierce fight with the Confederates before they withdrew. The Confederates only had 12 casualties in Battery Wagner.

A *Harper's Weekly* engraving of Brigadier General Quincy A. Gillmore. *Author's Collection.*

Over the next six days, Gillmore established four Union batteries with a total of 40 guns on Morris Island. Battery Wagner held a garrison of 1,300 men commanded by Brigadier General William B. Taliaferro.

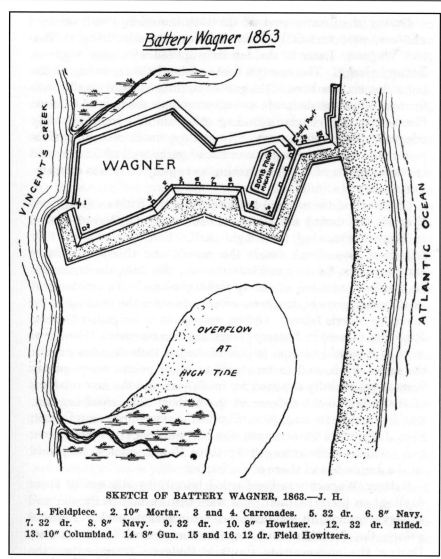

SKETCH OF BATTERY WAGNER, 1863.—J. H.

1. Fieldpiece. 2. 10" Mortar. 3 and 4. Carronades. 5. 32 dr. 6. 8" Navy. 7. 32 dr. 8. 8" Navy. 9. 32 dr. 10. 8" Howitzer. 12. 32 dr. Rifled. 13. 10" Columbiad. 14. 8" Gun. 15 and 16. 12 dr. Field Howitzers.

An engraving of Confederate Battery Wagner on Morris Island in 1863. *Courtesy of Willis J. Keith.*

On July 18 at 10:00 am, the Union batteries opened an intense bombardment of Battery Wagner, firing an average of 14 shells per minute. By 5:00 pm, the *Montauk* came within 300 yards of Battery Wagner on the high tide to join the attack. She was soon joined by the *New Ironsides*. After 10 continuous hours of bombardment, firing more than 9,000 shells, Gillmore ordered a second infantry attack on Battery Wagner.

Gillmore placed Brigadier General Thomas Seymour in command of 6,000 troops organized in three brigades. The attack would be led by Brigadier General George Strong commanding six regiments in the first brigade. The second brigade with four regiments was commanded by Colonel Haldiman S. Putnam and Brigadier General T. G. Stevenson commanded the third brigade. Putnam did not agree with the plan for the frontal assault and he commented to a junior officer that "we are going into Wagner like a flock of sheep."

Brigadier General George C. Strong. *Author's Collection.*

At dusk, the 54th Massachusetts, commanded by Colonel Robert Shaw, led Strong's brigade in the attack. They were supported by the 9th Maine and 76th Pennsylvania in the main column and the 6th Connecticut right flank and the 3rd New Hampshire and 48th New York on the left flank. As they neared the battery, guns from Fort Sumter, Battery Gregg and James Island opened fire.

With the first brigade experiencing heavy losses, Putnam's brigade was ordered to advance, but he stalled for 15 minutes before complying. Shaw, climbing the parapet at Wagner, challenged his men to "take the fort or die." By this time, all of the commanding officers in the first brigade were either killed or wounded. A general retreat was ordered for the Union troops but many of them had penetrated the Confederate battery and were engaged in fierce hand-to-hand combat. This continued until the Union troops at the battery were killed, wounded or captured.

Lieutenant Daniel West, 6th Connecticut Infantry, later wrote:

> *I had been in several battles before in Virginia . . . but nothing in my experience compared with the slaughter in front and in Fort Wagner that night . . . The dead and wounded covered it [the seaward wall]*

so that it was impossible to get around. All of our commanding officers were either killed or disabled.

By 10:30 pm, that attack was over, leaving a horrific scene in its wake. The Union army suffered more than 1,500 casualties, including 111 officers. Colonel Shaw was killed in the attack and Brigadier General Strong died of his wounds 12 days later. The Confederate casualties only totaled less than 200.

Frank Vizetelly, a correspondent for the Illustrated London News, was at Battery Wagner to witness the fight. He reported to his readers:

> *All through the night we could hear the screams and groans of the wounded lying within a few yards of us; but as a continual fire was kept up by the advanced pickets it was impossible to do anything for them without running great risk of being shot. Early in the morning, however, the Federals sent a flag of truce, asking for a cessation of hostilities, that they might bury their dead. The first demand was granted, but they were told they could not be permitted to come within the lines of the Confederates and the latter would perform the last offices for the fallen enemy. In the ditch they lay piled, Negroes and whites, four and five deep on each other; there could not have been less than 250 in the moat, some partially submerged; and altogether over 600 were buried by the Southerners.*

A soldier in Battery Wagner with the 32nd Georgia Infantry described the scene on Sunday morning:

> *I never saw such a sight as presented itself on Sunday morning at day brake [sic] – as far as the eye could reach could be seen the dead and dying on all sides . . . I never saw such a sight, men with heads off, many with legs shot off . . .*

With this second defeat at the hands of Battery Wagner, it was clear that Gillmore would not be able to force a speedy surrender of Charleston and he prepared siege operations on Morris Island. Union troops began a slow advance by digging zigzag trenches to advance on Battery Wagner. Gillmore also ordered the Union batteries on Morris Island to turn their attention to Fort Sumter.

Beauregard and his district engineer, Lt. Colonel D. B. Harris, planned to fill the casemates at Fort Sumter with wet sand and bales of cotton soaked in salt water to support the walls. The work on site was supervised by Lieutenant John Johnson, the engineer at the fort. Beauregard also transferred 20 of Fort Sumter's guns to James Island and around the inner harbor defenses. Colonel Alfred Rhett, Confederate commander at Fort Sumter, prepared his garrison for the attack they assumed would come.

On August 17, 1863, Union Battery Brown fired on Fort Sumter with two 8-inch Parrott rifles, one firing solid shot and the other percussion shells. Other batteries joined in, bringing 18 guns to bear on Fort Sumter. By mid-morning, the monitors *Passaic* and *Patapsco* joined in the attack. In the first 24 hours of the Fort Sumter bombardment, 1,000 shells were fired by the Union army and navy. At Fort Sumter, seven guns were disabled and the walls suffered heavy damage.

Colonel Robert Shaw, commander of the 54th Massachusetts Volunteer Infantry. *Author's Collection.*

The bombardment continued each day. The walls of Fort Sumter could not withstand the force of the heavy rifled Parrott guns Gillmore was using for the bombardment. By August 21, the Confederate guns at Fort Sumter were not returning fire. Gillmore sent a message to Beauregard that unless Confederate troops were withdrawn from Morris Island and Fort Sumter, he would fire on the city of Charleston. Beauregard refused and at 1:30 am on August 22, the Swamp Angel fired its first shot into the port city.

The Swamp Angel was a "floating battery" constructed in the marsh between Morris Island and James Island. Colonel Edward Serrell, an engineer with the 1st New York, designed a parapet of logs and sandbags surrounding a gun platform holding a large Parrott gun that could fire 150-pound shells. To build the parapet, soldiers had to carry more than 13,000 sandbags weighing over 800 tons across a wooden plank causeway that was 2 feet wide and 1,700 feet long.

Assault on Battery Wagner, July 18, 1863, published in the *Illustrated London News*. *Author's Collection*.

The southern slope of the ditch surrounding Battery Wagner, published in the *Illustrated London News. Author's Collection.*

The Swamp Angel on August 22, 1863, after the gun burst. *Courtesy of the Library of Congress.*

Once completed, the platform took 20,000 feet of wooden planking cut from the pine forest on Folly Island, 600 pounds of iron spikes and the equivalent of 10,000 man days of labor. One Union soldier remarked, "We're building a pulpit on which a Swamp Angel will preach." The gun was elevated to an extreme angle to enable the shells to reach Charleston, 7,900 yards away.

As the first shot from the Swamp Angel landed in Charleston, Vizetelly was lying awake in his bed reading a book on the Battle of Waterloo. He first considered that "a high meteor had fallen." Minutes later, a second shot landed in the city. Vizetelly wrote of that night:

> *The population was now aroused, the streets filled with women and children making their way to the upper part of the city, where they would find comparative safety. The volunteer fire-brigades brought out their engines, and parties of the citizen reserves were organized rapidly and quietly, to be in readiness to give assistance where required. The first engine that reached the house struck by the first shell was one belonging to a Negro company, and at it they went with a will, subduing the fire in a marvelously short time. At every succes-*
> *sive whirr about them the niggers shouted quaint invectives against "cussed bobolitionists," scattering for shelter until the danger was passed. Through the streets I went, and down to the Battery promenade, meeting on my way sick and bed-ridden people carried from their homes on mattresses, and mothers with infants in their arms running they knew not whither. Reaching the promenade, I cast my eyes towards the Federal position, and presently beyond James Island, across a marsh that separates it from Morris Island, came a flash, then a dull report and, after an interval of some seconds, a frightful rushing sound above me told the path the shell had taken; its flight must have been five miles!*

After two hours of constant shelling, the firing slowed and near dawn stopped. During the long night, 10 incendiary and six explosive shells were fired into Charleston. Exhausted, Vizetelly and many of the other guests at the hotel went to bed. That morning, English, French and Spanish consuls that were stationed in Charleston sent dispatches to Gillmore. They vehemently objected to the firing on innocent women and children in Charleston. Gillmore indicated that the shelling would continue, but he would give anyone left in Charleston the next 24 hours to clear the city.

The next day, the firing from the Swamp Angel continued as promised by Gillmore. Finally, upon the 36th shot fired from the elevated Parrott gun, the barrel could no longer withstand the pressure, and the Swamp Angel burst.

After the firing ceased, Vizetelly wrote:

> *It was now that, foiled at all points and smarting under his failures, the Federal general was guilty of that barbarity which has disgraced him as a soldier. Unable to capture the forts…he intimated that unless they were surrendered, he would turn his powerful guns upon the city. The threat was disregarded–disbelieved in, no doubt…in violation of warfare, he turned his guns on unoffending women and children.*

On day six of the bombardment on Fort Sumter, five monitors anchored 800 yards away and fired on the fort. Fire was returned by Confederate batteries on Sullivan's Island and Battery Gregg at Cummings Point on Morris Island. Two days later, Gillmore wrote General Halleck in Washington, "Fort Sumter is today a shapeless and harmless mass of ruins." He had fired more than 5,000 shots against Fort Sumter to reduce the fort to rubble.

On September 1, six monitors assembled to attack Fort Sumter. They moved in a single file with the *Weehawken* leading the way. By 11:30 am, the monitors were within 500 yards on the Confederate fort. At this point, the batteries on Sullivan's Island opened fire on the ships. Joined by the *New Ironsides*, the Union ships bombarded Fort Sumter for five hours firing more than 240 shots and hitting the fort 71 times. The east wall of Fort Sumter suffered great damage. Some shells passed completely through the fort to hit the west wall.

As the Union trenches were now dangerously close to Battery Wagner, Beauregard was fearful of losing his troops there and at Battery Gregg. On the night of September 6, the Confederate

troops evacuated Morris Island by boat. The Confederates at Battery Wagner defiantly held their position for 58 days, facing a Union army more than ten times their number and a fleet of armored vessels. At 5:10 am, Gillmore signaled to Dahlgren, "The whole island is ours, but the enemy have escaped us."

At Fort Sumter, with no large guns operational, the fort was nothing more than an infantry outpost. Colonel Rhett was transferred to command inner harbor fortifications and Beauregard placed Major Stephen Elliott in command at Fort Sumter notifying him:

> *You are to be sent to a fort deprived of all offensive capability, and having but one gun – a 32-pounder – with which to salute the flag,*

The first shell from the Swamp Angel exploding in Charleston, published in the *Illustrated London News. Author's Collection.*

morning and evening. But that fort is Fort Sumter, the key to the entrance of this harbor. It must be held to the bitter end: not with artillery, as heretofore, but with infantry alone; and there can be no hope of reinforcements.

Union Battery Hays, a breaching battery of Fort Sumter. *Courtesy of the Library of Congress.*

Fresh troops, 320 in number, were rotated to Fort Sumter. Understanding that he may soon face an amphibious assault on the fort, Elliott obtained a supply of hand grenades and fireballs for his defense. He also placed wire and other obstructions at the tops of his crumbled walls to help thwart any attempt to cross over.

Given that Fort Sumter had no operable guns, Dahlgren demanded that Elliott surrender Fort Sumter, to which he responded, "Inform Admiral Dahlgren that he may have Fort Sumter when he can take it and hold it." Accepting the challenge, Dahlgren planned an amphibious assault. He assigned Commander T. H. Stevens to lead the attack, telling him, "There is nothing but a corporal's guard at the fort and all we have to do is go in and take it."

The relationship between the Union army and navy was never a great one as jealousies and egos collided, and by September 1863, the relationship between Gillmore and Dahlgren was at a breaking point. Both Gillmore and Dahlgren planned amphibious assaults on Fort Sumter. Gillmore proposed that they collaborate but under army command. After Dahlgren refused, Gillmore

withdrew his support and participation for a joint assault and planned his own assault.

On the night of September 8, 500 Union sailors and marines boarded small boats and were towed to within 400 yards of Fort Sumter. From there they rowed to the fort for the assault. Elliott and 300 troops from the Charleston Battalion watched as the assault force neared. As the Union assault force neared the southeastern and southern faces of the fort, they were expecting nothing more than token resistance.

Elliott ordered his men to hold fire until the Union force was within yards of the fort. They then greeted the sailors and marines with a barrage of musket

The exterior of Fort Sumter showing the damage of the 1863 bombardments. Note the chevaux-de-frise at the top. *Courtesy of the Library of Congress.*

FORT SUMTER NATIONAL MONUMENT *"Where the Civil War Began"*

fire, hand grenades and fireballs. The Confederate gunboat *Chicora*, positioned nearby, opened fire on the Union attackers, as did the guns at Fort Moultrie and Fort Johnson. Taking on intense fire, the supporting Union ships withdrew, abandoning the sailors and marines on the rocks at the fort. That night, 124

Fort Putnam on Morris Island. *Courtesy of the Library of Congress.*

"The Evening Gun at Fort Sumter," painted by Confederate soldier Conrad Wise Chapman. *Courtesy of the Museum of the Confederacy.*

of Dahlgren's men were killed, wounded or captured and four boats were lost. Gilmore's men never arrived at Fort Sumter. The low tide on the night of the 8th kept them detained at Morris Island. Clearly, they had miscalculated both the ability and the determination of the small Confederate garrison at Fort Sumter.

In the rest of September, the Union batteries and gunboats gave Fort Sumter scant attention. Dahlgren was leery of attempting another ironclad attack knowing that the firepower at Fort Moultrie had been increased. Gillmore concentrated on rebuilding and arming the captured Confederate positions at Battery Wagner and Battery Gregg. Gillmore continued to build his army, accumulating 22,000 troops on Morris, Folly and Kiawah Islands by the end of September 1863.

Completing his buildup on Morris Island, he renamed the captured batteries. Battery Wagner was renamed Fort Strong, in honor of Union Brigadier General George Strong who died of his injuries on the July 18 assault on the battery. Battery Gregg was renamed Fort Putnam, in honor of brigade commander Colonel Haldiman Putnam, killed in the same attack.

In October 1863, the Confederates began remounting some of the guns at Fort Sumter. On October 26, Gillmore opened fire on Fort Sumter from Forts Strong and Putnam. Dahlgren supported the attack with fire from the *Patapsco* and *Lehigh*. This action began the second great bombardment of Fort Sumter which would last for 41 days.

One soldier wrote of daily life in the fort during this time:

All that we can see is the bursting of shells, and the flying of bricks, and fragments of shells through the air, and our sole thought is how to keep out of the way of them. The continued cry of the sentinels "Look out" from the parapet continuously in the ear, until every sound seems to bear the same refrain. On yesterday one of the sentinels on post was literally torn into pieces by a shell. Poor fellow he never knew what hit him!

Most of the top of Fort Sumter's walls and the gorge wall were cut down. The Confederate garrison grew concerned about another amphibious assault as the debris fell outward from the fort, leaving the fort vulnerable to a breach. Theodore Honour, a private with the Washington Light Infantry, wrote in his journal, "The sea-face to the fort is completely demolished, and in its stead is an incline of rubbish that will make it no difficult matter for the Yanks to land, and try by a desperate charge to fain entrance to the fort, but we are here to defend that weak spot."

On October 31, 13 men with the Washington Light Infantry were killed at Fort Sumter when a Union shell forced the collapse of a roof that fell on them. Honour also recorded the events of that day:

"The Flag at Fort Sumter," October 20, 1863, painted by Confederate soldier Conrad Wise Chapman. *Courtesy of the Museum of the Confederacy.*

The firing from the batteries on Morris Island all day and night was terrific; nothing like it since the last days of Battery Wagner, and we were certain that it would culminate in an attack in barges. The firing from the land batteries together with the enfilading fire from the iron clads kept up one continued roar of cannon & mortars, and it was estimated that 1,000 shot & shells were fired at the fort. It was computed by us that for some time two shells a minute burst inside the fort. At dark our Grenade corps was ordered by Maj. Elliott to get our hand grenades and boxes of Greek fire as near to the parapet of the fort as possible, as it was expected after the heavy bombardment the enemy would make an assault in their barges.

The walls & parapet of the fort was in such a condition as to almost make it impossible to find a place where we could go with the grenades. Maj. Elliott told me to take the men into a casemate on the north side of the fort, and I went first to investigate, and as I got to the entrance of the room a 300-pound Parrot shell from the battery at Cummings Point burst in the room killing 3 negroes who had taken refuge there thinking it a place of safety. Of course that was no place for us, and so I reported to Maj. Elliott who then told me to take a casemate on the ground tier at the foot of the iron staircase, and wait there. When I got there, I found the room occupied by a detachment of Company A (WLI's) and some of the Georgia 12th Battalion as sleeping quarters. We then determined to place the grenades & Greek fire in the "bombproof" for safe keeping and take our chances where we could.

About midnight, a shell from a 300-pound Parrott from the battery on Morris Island or perhaps from one of the iron clads struck the end of the main girder to the room in which our men were sleeping and on which rested hundreds of tons of debris & old iron from the demolished east face of the fort, fell in upon the sleeping men. In an instant of time the WLI's Company A had lost 13 of their men, crushed with the falling of the rubbish. Only one man of our company then in the room – I. I. Petit – escaped and his escape was miraculous. He was standing inside the door looking out (not being able to sleep) and saw the wall totter, and some dirt fall, and sprang through the door nor stopped until he was 50 feet off, and thus saved his life. Lawrence, Fred, and I were sitting together talking and looking out of a room to the south of the fort when the crash came and we immediately sprang out with the rest of the garrison to try and save if possible some of our poor fellows. Lawrence soon had a crowd of Negroes working like heroes getting the rubbish away from those that had been crushed nearest the outer walls. After working for some time with the shells bursting around them they succeeded in getting to where the dead laid crushed, with no sign of life.

On many days during the bombardment that lasted into December more than 1,000 shots were fired onto Fort Sumter. Many of the Union guns were bursting from constant and repetitive use. With no large guns left in Fort Sumter capable of responding, the Confederate batteries on James and Sullivan's Islands fired on the Morris Island Federal positions. During this period, the Confederate troops in Fort Sumter never numbered more than 300. A Confederate ironclad and row boats staged at Fort Johnson and Sullivan's Island were ready to help defend against any attempt at another amphibious assault.

At 3:00 am on November 30, 250 Union troops on barges were spotted approaching Fort Sumter. The garrison opened fire once the invaders were within 300 yards. After the guns at Sullivan's Island and Fort Johnson also opened fire, the barges withdrew.

Finally, after December 6, after firing more than 18,000 shots on the beleaguered Confederate outpost, the daily bombardment on Fort Sumter subsided. The garrison could now move within the fort to make some minor improvements to their crumbling defenses. The parade ground was cleared. Gabions, wicker baskets filled with sand, were placed on the crumbling walls of the fort. A three-gun battery was mounted on the northeast face of Fort Sumter designed to keep any Union ship from making a run to the inner harbor. A 275-foot underground tunnel was constructed within the fort.

On the morning of December 11, 1863, a great explosion at Fort Sumter killed 11 men and wounded 41 others. The explosion started an intense fire in the

The breach on the north wall at Fort Sumter, patched with gabions. *Courtesy of the Library of Congress.*

fort's tunnels. Seeing trouble at the fort, all the Union batteries on Morris Island opened fire, sending more than 200 shots onto the burning fort. The Confederate batteries on Sullivan's Island opened fire on Fort Putnam to assist Fort Sumter.

Elliott had the band at Fort Sumter strike up "Dixie" to let everyone, Confederate and Union, know that all was well in the rubble fort. The Union soldiers terminated their firing and cheered the brave and determined men at Fort Sumter.

The official report stated that "fire from an accidental explosion of small-arms ammunition" set off the explosion." The "unofficial" word was that a candle burning too close to an open barrel of whiskey in the tunnel created the problem. Whatever the source of the explosion, with the fire underground, Elliott had no choice but to let the fire burn itself out.

After December 1863, firing on Fort Sumter was intermittent. There were no serious attempts to take the fort or advance on Charleston. In 1864, all possible Union troops were called to Virginia to support General Ulysses S. Grant's operations. On

Captain John C. Mitchel, commander of Fort Sumter, was mortally wounded by a shell fragment on July 20, 1864. On October 13, 1896, his mother presented Mitchel's sword and the flag flying over Fort Sumter on the day of his death to the City of Charleston. *Courtesy of Willis J. Keith.*

May 1, Gillmore and 18,000 troops departed South Carolina for Fort Monroe on the Virginia peninsula. Dahlgren's fleet was also reduced as some of the gunboats and the man-of-war *New Ironsides* departed for duty northward.

Later in May, Fort Sumter got a new commanding officer as Captain John C. Mitchel relieved Elliott. Mitchel was the son of the famous Irish nationalist John Mitchel who escaped to America and was later publisher of the *Southern Citizen,* the first paper to assert that slavery was not the cause of the war but used as a pretence.

Charleston harbor remained quiet until the summer of 1864. Union General Foster believed that Fort Sumter was strengthening. In writing Washington, he indicated his resolve to reduce the remaining walls at Fort Sumter and finally take the fort with an amphibious assault large enough to overwhelm the small numbers of Confederate defenders.

On July 7, 1864, at first light, the bombardment of Fort Sumter resumed, firing an average of 350 rounds a day. Every day, a portion

The interior of Fort Sumter with gabion reinforcements. *Courtesy of the Library of Congress.*

On the afternoon of July 20, Captain Mitchel climbed the western wall of the fort with his spyglass to note the position of the Federal ships for his daily report. A mortar shell from Morris Island burst overhead and a shell fragment tore into his hip. Mitchel died of his wounds four hours later. After Mitchel's death, Captain Thomas A. Huguenin was placed in command.

An 1864 sketch of the interior of Fort Sumter by a Confederate engineer. *Courtesy of the Library of Congress.*

The firing slowed in August as Foster's supply of ammunition was running low. Finally, in early September, the bombardment that started 60 days earlier stopped. More than 14,666 rounds were fired onto Fort Sumter, but with the same result as before. The situation in Charleston seemed to have reached a stalemate. Though firing would continue sporadically, this ended the last great bombardment of Fort Sumter.

An 1864 sketch of the interior of Fort Sumter by a Confederate engineer. *Courtesy of the Library of Congress.*

of the fort's wall was knocked down but it was only contributing to the enormous piles of debris. Each night, the Confederate troops and workmen went to work placing wire fencing and other entanglements on top of the rubble to discourage an amphibious assault. Union batteries tried to interfere with the nightly work by firing mortar rounds on the fort. At Fort Sumter, engineer Captain John Johnson requisitioned 1,000 bags of sand to be delivered each night. The sand with the masonry debris was capable of absorbing the concussion of the Union shells and actually making Fort Sumter stronger. By late July, Dahlgren felt that Fort Sumter was "nearly impregnable."

Quincy Adams Gillmore

Quincy A. Gillmore was born on February 25, 1825, in Black River, Lorain County, Ohio. He graduated first in his class at the United States Military Academy at West Point in 1849. He was commissioned into the Corps of Engineers and, from 1849 – 1852, worked on the construction of coastal fortifications at Hampton Roads, Virginia. Gilmore accepted a position as instructor of "Practical Military Engineering" at West Point from 1852 – 1856.

In 1856, Gillmore was promoted to first lieutenant and worked as a purchasing agent for the United States Army in New York. At the outset of the Civil War, he was assigned to Brigadier General Thomas W. Sherman's staff as a military engineer and promoted to captain.

Sherman decided to capture Fort Pulaski in Georgia before tackling the more difficult task of Charleston. Most Union and Confederate officers felt that Fort Pulaski was impregnable given that the nearest high ground on which siege guns could be placed was more than a mile away. Gillmore insisted that the new rifled guns were up to the task and he constructed 11 batteries beginning in December 1861. On April 10, 1862, the attack on Fort Pulaski began and by that afternoon the fort's walls were giving way to the powerful Federal guns. By noon on the second day, a large breach opened on the southeast face of the fort. Confederate Colonel Charles Olmstead surrendered Fort Pulaski on April 11 and Gillmore's reputation as a skilled military engineer became widely known.

On June 12, 1863, Gillmore, now a brigadier general, was given command of the Department of the South and he set his aim on Charleston. After establishing a foothold on Folly and Kiawah Islands, he moved his troops to capture the southern end of Morris Island. Though his ill-fated frontal assault on Battery Wagner on July 18, 1863, was a disaster, he was not widely criticized as were the failures of other Union officers before him. Unable to quickly take Morris Island or force the surrender of Charleston, the Union operations in the harbor settled into the longest siege of the Civil War.

Brigadier General Gillmore in front of his tent on Morris Island. *Courtesy of the Library of Congress.*

In May 1864, Gillmore and the X Corps were transferred to Virginia and participated in the failed Bermuda Hundred Campaign outside of Richmond. In July 1864, Gillmore organized a 20,000-man force to meet a threat from Confederate General Jubal A. Early, saving Washington from capture.

Gillmore returned to Charleston in January 1865, and was there for the Confederate evacuation of the city on February 17. On March 13, 1865, he was promoted to brevet major general in the U.S. Army.

After the Civil War, Gillmore accepted an assignment with the Army Corps of Engineers in Charleston. He designed a system of harbor jetties that, once in place, could keep a deep draft shipping channel scoured to acceptable depths. The work took 17 years and 3.7 million dollars to complete, but his design for the jetties also resulted in the erosion of Morris Island at the rate of 25 feet per year.

Stephen Elliot Jr.

Stephen Elliott Jr. was born in Beaufort in 1832, the son of Bishop Stephen Elliott, the first bishop of the Episcopal Church of Georgia. After South Carolina's secession, Elliott formed and equipped at light battery, later named the Beaufort Volunteer Artillery.

He was present for the bombardment of Fort Sumter but shortly after returned to the Beaufort District. He was a daring officer and was aggressive in his actions. In 1861, Elliott and 20 of his men set sail on a tug from Port Royal to capture a Union 1,200-ton sailing vessel offshore.

In the fall of 1861, Elliott was assigned to Bay Point at Port Royal Harbor. He commanded an artillery unit in Fort Beauregard during the one-day Battle of Port Royal on November 7. Once the Union army occupied the Beaufort District, Elliott and his men executed a series of raids on Union positions at area plantations. He also developed a floating torpedo which hit and sank a Federal tender in St. Helena Bay.

In early 1863, Elliott was promoted to Chief of Artillery for the Third Military District. He was promoted to major and then lieutenant colonel. Twice he led Confederate troops against Union troops near Pocotaligo.

Transferred to Fort Sumter, Elliott served under Colonel Alfred Rhett. After Rhett's transfer, Elliott was promoted to command the Charleston Battalion occupying Fort Sumter. When Union Admiral Dahlgren

Confederate Major (Brigadier General) Stephen Elliott. *Courtesy of Willis J. Keith.*

demanded the surrender of Fort Sumter in the fall of 1863, Elliott refused.

On September 8, Elliott and his men repulsed an amphibious assault on Fort Sumter by 500 Union sailors and marines. The Union Navy withdrew with 124 men killed, wounded or captured, while the Confederates suffered no casualties. From October 26 to December 6, Fort Sumter received the brunt of an intense bombardment, yet Elliott held his position, even as the fort crumbled around him. In May 1864, Captain John C. Mitchel relieved Elliott at Fort Sumter.

Elliott was sent to Petersburg, Virginia as an officer in Holcombe's Legion. On May 24, 1864, he was promoted to brigadier general and given command of the brigade formerly led by Nathan "Shanks" Evans for the defense of Petersburg.

Two of his regiments suffered severe losses when the Federal mine exploded on July 30, 1864, at what came to be called the Battle of the Crater. Elliott led his men in attacking the Union troops moving through the breach in the Confederate lines after the explosion. He was critically wounded and sent home to South Carolina to recover. Elliott died on March 21, 1866, from the lingering effects of his war wounds received at Petersburg. He is forever remembered as one of the valiant defenders of Fort Sumter.

A painting by Seth Eastman of the interior of Fort Sumter after the long Federal siege. *Courtesy of the Collection of the US House of Representatives.*

Anderson Returns

When General William T. Sherman marched out of Atlanta in November 1864, his next destination was the subject of great speculation by the Confederate command. The 5th Georgia was pulled from South Carolina and sent to Macon, Georgia. Brigadier General James Chesnut Jr. moved the South Carolina Reserves to Georgia as well. Confederate General Hardee, commanding troops in Charleston, was sent to Savannah. Major General Robert Ransom replaced Hardee in Charleston. Soon, it was determined that Sherman was marching to Savannah.

During the six weeks of Sherman's "march to the sea" in Georgia, little happened in Charleston. Even Fort Sumter was receiving little attention from the Federal artillerymen. Union General Hatch, on Morris Island, observed, "The battering of Sumter is, in my opinion, an idle waste of material . . ." General Halleck, in Washington, sent a dispatch to General Foster that General Grant "wanted the expenditure of ammunition upon Charleston and Fort Sumter discontinued."

In Georgia, Hardee evacuated Savannah on December 21, 1864, and Sherman, upon occupying the city, presented Savannah to President Lincoln as a Christmas present. While in Savannah, Sherman received a communiqué from General Halleck in Washington. Halleck stated:

> *Should you capture Charleston, I hope that by some accident the place may be destroyed, and if a little salt should be sown upon its site it may prevent the growth of future crops of nullification and secession.*

Having already decided to march on Columbia, Sherman replied:

> *I will bear in mind your hint as to Charleston and don't think salt will be necessary. When I move, the Fifteenth Corps will be on the right of the Right Wing, and their position will bring them naturally,*

> *into Charleston first; and if you have watched the history of that corps you will have remarked that they generally do their work up pretty well. The truth is the whole army is burning with insatiable desire to wreck vengeance upon South Carolina. I almost tremble at her fate.*

Sherman communicated to Foster in Hilton Head, "I regard any attempt to enter Charleston Harbor by its direct channel or to carry it by storm of James Island as too hazardous to warrant the attempt." However, Foster and Dahlgren periodically made a show of force to occupy the Confederate troops in Charleston, prohibiting their withdrawal to further reinforce any attempt to slow or stop Sherman's movements.

On the evening of January 15, 1865, Dahlgren dispatched the monitor *Patapsco* on patrol to look for harbor obstructions. While still 800 yards from Fort Sumter, she hit a mine and immediately sank. Sixty-two of the 105 man crew went down with the ship.

On January 30, 1865, Gillmore was ordered back to South Carolina to relieve Foster as commander of the Department of the South. At this time, Fort Sumter still had a garrison of 300 men from the 32nd Georgia Volunteers and two companies of the 1st South Carolina Artillery. The fort was still nothing more than an infantry outpost except for the three guns on the northeast face guarding the shipping channel.

On February 14, Beauregard sent instructions to evacuate Charleston. The Confederate troops were to travel by railroad through St. Stephens to Columbia and go to reinforce General Joseph E. Johnston in North Carolina. Union signalmen on Morris Island were intercepting messages from Charleston to the harbor forts regarding the pending evacuation.

On February 16, Major Thomas A. Huguenin, Confederate commander at Fort Sumter, received a telegraphic dispatch ordering that he prepare to leave the fort that had been so valiantly defended for 567 days. That same evening, he sent the sick, black laborers used by the engineers, servants and the garrison's personal baggage to Charleston.

This engraving published in *Frank Leslie's Illustrated News* depicts Captain H. M. Bragg of General Gillmore's staff, raising the United States flag after the Confederate evacuation of Fort Sumter. *Author's Collection.*

On the morning of February 17, a new Confederate flag was raised over Fort Sumter. The officers prepared their troops to leave the fort. At sunset, the flag was lowered and a salute fired. Near 10:00 pm, two steamers, commanded by Lieutenant Thomas L. Swinton, arrived at Fort Sumter to evacuate the garrison. The roll was called and the troops marched to the two ships. Major Huguenin, the commander; Lieutenant E. J. White, the fort's engineer; and Lieutenant W. G. Ogier, adjutant of the post, went to the ramparts and relieved the evening's sentinels, sending them to the boats.

In 1863, Huguenin was the last to depart Battery Wagner on its evacuation. On the night of February 17, 1865, he was now the last to leave Fort Sumter. He recorded his thoughts that night in his report:

> *After visiting every portion of the fort, with a heavy heart I reached the wharf, no one was left behind but many a heart clung to those sacred and battle scared ramparts, I cannot describe my emotions. I felt as if every tie held dear to me was about to be severed; the pride and glory of Sumter was there, and now in the gloom of darkness we were to abandon her, for whom every one of us would have shed the last drop of his blood.*

Lee Harby, a young woman in Charleston, wrote of the events in Charleston on the night of the 17th and the next morning:

> *It was a terrible, heart-breaking, awful night. The men who were garrisoning Sumter had come over in their small boats, bringing their flags. In the early morning of the 18th, they were gathered in the city on the wharf, and there they cast themselves down on the earth and wept aloud. Some prayed; some cursed; all said they would rather have died in the fort they had so long defended than have her ramparts desecrated by the invader's tread . . .*

On the morning of the 18th, believing that the Confederate troops were now gone, the USS *Canonicus* fired several shots onto Fort Moultrie, and received no reply. Major John A. Hennessy, of the 52nd Pennsylvania Infantry, departed Cummings Point on a small boar and was the first to arrive at Fort Sumter. Hennessy and the boat crew scaled the parapet and raised his regimental flag over Fort Sumter, the first federal flag to fly over the fort since April 14, 1861.

The siege on Fort Sumter and Charleston lasted 567 days, the longest siege of the Civil War. In that time, the Union army and navy fired 46,053 rounds of artillery on Fort Sumter. Despite the immense bombardment, the Confederate casualties at the fort numbered no more than 52 killed and 267 wounded. The

After the evacuation of Charleston, the 55th Massachusetts Volunteer Infantry, led by Colonel Augustus G. Bennett, marched through the streets of the city singing "The March of John Brown's Soul." *Author's Collection.*

small Confederate garrison stubbornly held their fort in the face of seemingly insurmountable odds. The defense of Fort Sumter, against a combined army and navy with superior numbers and superior firepower, ranks amongst the greatest in the history of warfare.

As Union troops entered the city of Charleston, they were accompanied by W. T. Crane, a war correspondent writing for *Frank Leslie's Illustrated News.* Crane wrote of his observations in Charleston:

> *The appearance baffles all description; scarcely a house remains intact; in some instances a dozen shell have entered the same building; its glass invariably shattered in almost every window; roofs are crushed and walls lean, crack, and gape at you as you silently and thoughtfully gaze upon them; grass is growing in the streets;…Crows scream around the ruins; broken bricks, timbers and debris of all kind are heaped around…Look at it now, and we see the blight of the touch of secession's fingers.*

Secretary of War Edwin M. Stanton was elated over the fall of Charleston and, in March, issued the following order on behalf of President Lincoln:

> *At the hour of noon, on the 14th day of April, 1865, Brevet Major-General Anderson will raise and plant upon the ruins of Fort Sumter, in Charleston harbor, the same United States flag which floated over the battlements of that fort during the rebel assault, and which was lowered and saluted by him, and the small force of*

his command, when the works were evacuated on the 14th of April, 1861.

Anderson agreed to attend but his wife, an invalid, could not make the long journey. He and his six-year-old son traveled to Charleston by ship. Many traveled from the northern states for the ceremony and the opportunity to tour Charleston in its ruinous state. In New York, the Neptune Steamship Company chartered the steamship *Oceanus* to travel to Charleston and sold tickets for $100 a piece.

As steamships loaded with celebrants neared Charleston Harbor, they were

On February 21, Gillmore, his staff and guests toured the ruins of Fort Sumter as depicted in this 1865 *Harper's Weekly* engraving. *Author's Collection.*

greeted by the Rattlesnake Shoals lightship, marking the channel in the absence of the Morris Island Lighthouse, destroyed by the Confederate authorities in 1861. Passing Morris, Sullivan's and James Islands, ships' captains familiar with the harbor narrated the sites as they passed that most passengers had read of so frequently during the war. Aboard the *Oceanus*, as they passed Fort Sumter, one passenger noted:

> *Involuntarily, our heads are all uncovered.*
> *A solemn silence pervades the throng, as*
> *for a moment the thought of the past four*
> *years, with their changes, passions, carnage,*
> *suffering, defeats, depression, and final*
> *triumph flashes through every mind . . . by a*
> *common inspiration, our voices break forth in*
> *one grand, surging, heaven-echoed chorus:*
> *"Praise God, from whom all blessings flow!*
> *Praise Him, all creatures here below!*
> *Praise Him above, ye Heavenly Host!*
> *Praise Father, Son, and Holy Ghost!"*

On the morning of April 14, a crowd of more than 5,000 people booked passage to Fort Sumter. The wharf at the fort was lined with a company of soldiers "with muskets shouldered and bayonets fixed – on the left, white, on the right, black, rivaling each other in soldierly bearing."

Wooden steps were constructed over the wall to allow entrance to the fort. A new flagstaff was erected on the parade ground for the day's ceremony. Abner Doubleday, Norman Hall and Peter Hart who served at Fort Sumter with Robert Anderson were in attendance.

Opening the ceremony was Reverend Matthias Harris, the army chaplain with Anderson on December 27, 1860 who offered the first prayer on the raising of the colors. He stepped forward, removed his hat and offered a prayer for the day. He was followed by Reverend R. S. Storrs Jr., of Brooklyn, New York, who read passages from Psalms 20, 47, 98 and 126.

Brevet Brigadier General E. D. Townsend, assistant adjutant general, read a copy of Anderson's report written from the USS *Baltic* on April 18, 1861, after

The Federal Squadron anchored outside Fort Sumter on April 14, 1865. *Courtesy of the Library of Congress.*

the evacuation of Fort Sumter. Anderson then stepped to the podium and in an emotion filled address, spoke to the large gathering:

> *I am here, my friends, my fellow-citizens and fellow-soldiers, to*
> *perform an act of duty to my country dear to my heart, and which*
> *all of you will appreciate and feel. Had I observed the wishes of my*
> *heart it should be done in silence; but in accordance with the request*
> *of the Honorable Secretary of War, I make a few remarks, as by his*
> *order, after four long, long years of war; I restore to its proper place*
> *this dear flag, which I floated here during peace before the first act*
> *of this cruel rebellion. I thank God that I lived to see this day, and to*
> *be here, to perform this, perhaps the last act of my life, of duty to my*

The crowd awaiting the start of the ceremony on April 14, 1865. *Courtesy of the Library of Congress.*

country. My heart is filled with gratitude to that God who has so singly blessed us, who has given us blessings beyond measure. May all the nations bless and praise the name of the Lord, and all the world proclaim, Glory to God in the highest, and on earth peace, good-will toward men.

As he stepped to the flagstaff, he was met by Peter Hart. Hart reached into the original Fort Sumter mailbag and held up the flag which was removed from Fort Sumter on April 14, 1861, for all to see, to the roars of the crowd. He offered the flag to Anderson who was so overwhelmed that he could not raise the flag alone. With the help of Hart and several sailors there, the old, tattered flag was raised to the top of the 150-foot-tall flagstaff. The band played "The Star-Spangled Banner" as the crowd wept and hugged. A 100-gun salute was fired from Fort Sumter. This was followed by another salute fired from the former Confederate batteries surrounding the harbor.

Next, Reverend Henry Ward Beecher offered a lengthy address which he opened with:

On this solemn and joyful day, we again lift to the breeze, our father's flag, now, again the banner of the United States, with the fervent prayer that God would crown it with honor, protect it from treason, and send it down to our children, with all the blessings of civilization, liberty and religion. Terrible in battle, may it be beneficent in peace.

At the conclusion of Beecher's address, the crowd rose to sing The Doxology. The benediction was offered by Reverend Storrs Jr.

At 6:00 pm, a great banquet was given by General Hatch, commander of the Federal troops now

Fort Sumter viewed from the sandbar in 1865. *Courtesy of the Library of Congress.*

occupying Charleston. A multitude of speeches and toasts were offered during the celebratory dinner. The final toast of the evening was reserved for Robert Anderson. After his introductory remarks, he raised his glass and offered:

> *I beg you now, that you will join me in drinking to the health of another man whom we all love to honor, the man who, when elected President of the United States, was compelled to reach the seat of government with an escort, but now could travel all over the country with millions of hands and hearts to sustain him. I give you the good, the great, the honest man, Abraham Lincoln.*

As all in the hall joined in the toast, they were unaware that evening, in Washington, D.C., at Ford's Theater, John Wilkes Booth fired the fateful shot at the head of President Abraham Lincoln.

Thomas A Huguenin

Thomas A. Huguenin was born at Roseland Plantation in Christ Church Parish near Beaufort on November 18, 1839. He graduated from The Citadel with high honors and after receiving his diploma, was made assistant professor of mathematics. In 1860, he traveled to Europe to further his studies in military science.

Huguenin volunteered for service with state troops in January 1861, and was commissioned as a first lieutenant in Company A, 1st Regiment of Infantry. He was in Charleston for the bombardment of Fort Sumter on April 12, 1861. In May, he accepted a commission as first lieutenant in Confederate service and by July was promoted to captain.

In 1863, Huguenin was posted at Fort Moultrie and, later, chief of artillery at Morris Island from September 4 – 7. He was wounded on September 5 and again on September 6 as Battery Wagner was under intense fire. On the night of September 6, the Confederate troops evacuated Morris Island and Huguenin commanded the rear guard, consisting of 25 artillerymen and 10 sharpshooters. He supervised the men as they spiked the guns in the battery and ignited a slow fuse leading to the powder magazine. The last Confederate to leave Morris Island, he waded out to a waiting launch and made his escape before the Union troops discovered the evacuation.

After the death of Captain John C. Mitchel on July 20, 1864, Huguenin was given command of Fort Sumter. While commanding the fort, he was twice wounded in August and November. Huguenin held this post until the evacuation of Fort Sumter on February 17, 1865.

After the war, Huguenin returned to Christ Church Parish and worked to cultivate his land. In 1883, South Carolina Governor Hugh Smith Thompson gave Huguenin a commission as general to command the 4th Brigade of the South Carolina Militia. In 1894, Governor "Pitchfork" Ben Tillman ordered the 4th Brigade to Darlington to suppress a riot, when local citizens clashed with Dispensary constables over an enforcement of the state's liquor laws. Huguenin believed the riot was caused by the Dispensary constables and would not order his men to protect them. Tillman relieved him of command and into retirement.

General Huguenin lived out his last years in Charleston and died on February 27,

Major Thomas Huguenin, the last Confederate soldier to evacuate Fort Sumter. *Courtesy of the Library of Congress.*

1897, after an illness of several months. Regaled by Charlestonians as one of the heroes of Battery Wagner and Fort Sumter, he was buried at Magnolia Cemetery with military honors.

An aerial view of Fort Sumter. *Photograph taken by Buddy Moffet.*

Rising from the Ruins

In April 1865, Fort Sumter was in shambles. Only portions of the five walls remained standing. Sand, pulverized brick and dirt covered the gorge and right flank walls. The fort, in its post-war condition, was of little use. A temporary light was placed atop the walls as a navigation aid until a more permanent light could be constructed.

In August 1868, Captain William Ludlow surveyed the condition of Fort Sumter to determine the scope of work to render the site useable. General Gillmore, now with the Army Corps of Engineers, had plans drawn to place 28 casemates on reconstructed walls.

His plans were to only use the foundation of the original fort. As in the original plan, the gorge wall would house the living quarters for the garrison. The plan was similar to the original 1828 plan but the new walls would be constructed of granite.

No action was taken on Gillmore's proposal. A different plan for Fort Sumter was created by the Board of Engineers for Fortifications and approved in 1870 by Brigadier General A. A. Humphreys, Chief of Engineers and Secretary of War William Belnap. This plan called for 13 guns to be placed atop the ruins of the fort as a temporary measure to afford protection for the harbor. The walls would be leveled and parapets constructed to protect the gun emplacements. Interestingly, no plans were approved for the construction of any living quarters.

A budget of $44,000 was approved and Gillmore was in charge of the project with Captain Ludlow supervising the work at the fort. Bricks and timbers were salvaged at the fort for use in the new construction and a new wharf was built at the fort's entrance. Before much progress was made, work was suspended in 1871 when all the resources of the Army Corps of Engineers was re-directed to clearing the main shipping channel coming into the harbor.

Fort Sumter with palmetto log reinforcements on the channel side. *Courtesy of the Library of Congress.*

By the summer of 1872, Ludlow had partially excavated the debris and earth down to the foundation. Eight of the right face casemates were cleared but only three were in good condition. The damaged walls were reduced to a lower height, removing the third tier. The fort was armed with eleven 100-pound Parrott rifles located in the first tier gun rooms that were restored. Four eight-inch Parrott rifles and two 15-inch Rodman smoothbores were also installed at the fort.

While work was progressing, a storm passed through in the fall of 1874 that flooded the parade ground and damaged the re-built right flank wall. Since the

Exterior of Fort Sumter. *Courtesy of the Library of Congress.*

In December 1871, new plans were drawn for 10 "King's Depressing Carriages" to be mounted atop the walls. These new carriages, developed by Captain Rufus King Jr., held the guns in a lowered position for protection. The guns would be raised for firing and lowered again for reloading, providing greater protection for the gun crew. Work resumed in January 1872, although Gillmore did not plan to use the "depressing carriages" due to the high cost. Gillmore did propose to excavate the casemates for later use, though only the excavation of the right wall was approved.

The temporary lighthouse beacon placed at Fort Sumter in 1865. *Courtesy of the Library of Congress.*

A range light on Morris Island. *Courtesy of the National Archives.*

cisterns were now flooded with salt water, new cisterns were built above the level of the parade grounds to avoid future salt water intrusion. By early June 1876, a shortage of funds made it necessary to suspend work on the fort.

The original navigational aids guiding ships through the shipping channel to Charleston consisted of a "first-order" lighthouse and several range lights on Morris Island, a navigational light on Fort Sumter, lights at Castle Pinckney and a final light at the Battery in the city. In 1861, none of these lights existed as all were either destroyed or removed during the war.

The Fort Sumter light was a white light in a fifth-order Fresnel lens, completed in 1857. In December 1860, Governor Pickens extinguished all of the navigational lights in the harbor except Fort Sumter since the fort was not under his control. When the Confederate forces occupied Fort Sumter in April 1861, the light was removed. Once Union forces re-occupied the fort in February 1865, a temporary light was installed atop the battered wall.

With peace restored, the Lighthouse Service made plans to rebuild the lighthouse system in Charleston Harbor. Surveys of the harbor revealed that the deep channels had shifted. There were now two channels available to deep-draft ships: the Pumpkin Hill Channel and a South Channel. With the all

Ripley Shoal Lighthouse. *Author's Collection.*

of the lights and main lighthouse destroyed, Congress appropriated $15,000 in March 1867 to establish range lights on Morris Island. Like at Fort Sumter, a 35-foot skeleton frame beacon was constructed on Morris Island, south of the intended site for the new main lighthouse. The lighthouse tender *Maggie* was also assigned to the Charleston channel to augment the beacons. A beacon was installed on the Battery with a sixth order Fresnel lens as the terminus for the shipping channel.

The Lighthouse Service approved the hiring of one keeper to maintain the two beacons on Morris Island. Mr. C. K. Smith was hired at the rate of $100 per month and subsistence of $1 per day while in the field. In 1869, the Battery beacon was replaced with a beacon in the steeple of St. Philip's Church to relocate the beacon directly on line with the shipping channel. By the early 1870s, more permanent beacons were erected at the key harbor locations. Two beacons were constructed on Morris Island in 1870 and 1872, each equipped with a fifth order Fresnel lens. Between 1872 and 1876, beacons were constructed on Sullivan's Island. A permanent beacon was built at Fort Sumter, once again equipped with a fifth order lens. One beacon with a sixth order lens was first located at Fort Moultrie and, later, by 1879, re-established outside the fort. The second light, a rear beacon, had a fourth order Fresnel light. The beacon at Castle Pinckney was rebuilt with a fifth order Fresnel lens.

Fort Sumter with the new lighthouse. *Author's Collection.*

As the shipping channel shifted, the light at The Battery was replaced with a new light in the steeple of St. Philip's Episcopal Church. *Author's Collection.*

With beacons and a lightship in place, attention was turned to the main lighthouse intended for Morris Island. On March 3, 1873, Congress appropriated $60,000 for "commencing the rebuilding of a first order seacoast light on Morris Island destroyed during the war." This first appropriation allowed the engineering assessments to begin. Major Peter C. Hains, the chief engineer for the South Carolina lighthouse district, picked the logical site for the lighthouse to be constructed based on soil conditions and the relationship to the current shipping channel.

The remnants of Battery Huger at Fort Sumter, photographed in 1958. *Courtesy of the Library of Congress.*

Work on driving the piles for the main lighthouse commenced in the fall of 1873. In December 1873, Hains received a telegram from Washington requesting that work on the Morris Island lighthouse cease. Hains successfully defended the importance of the project stating, "I would also call your attention to the importance of this lighthouse. Charleston is rapidly becoming one of the most important ports of entry for large ships engaged in the cotton trade. There is no seacoast light between Cape Romain and Tybee Island, a distance of about 100 miles."

In March 1875, Congress passed the final appropriation of $30,000 to complete the Morris Island lighthouse. The lantern was outfitted with a first order Fresnel

A view of Fort Sumter National Monument from Charleston Harbor. *Photograph by Bryan Riggs.*

lens, the latest technology, and the proper-sized light for a seacoast lighthouse. The lens had more than one thousand individual prisms and weighed more than twelve thousand, eight hundred pounds. These Fresnel lenses were a major investment as a first order lens in 1873 cost $10,000. The lens for Morris Island was fixed white with an arc of two hundred seventy degrees. It had a visibility of nineteen miles out to sea. The Morris Island Lighthouse was first illuminated on October 1, 1876.

With work complete on the main lighthouse, attention was directed, once again, to the harbor beacons. In 1877, construction to locate a beacon at Fort Ripley, an interior harbor fort built in 1862 on Middle Ground Shoal, located between the Battery and the northern shore on James Island. A fifth order Fresnel lens was installed, 51 feet above mean high tide. The lens initially operated with a fixed white light, changed in the twentieth century to a fixed red light. The structure also operated a fog bell, sounding every ten seconds.

The lighthouse at Fort Sumter was 51 feet tall and fitted with a fifth order Fresnel lens. It also used a bell as a mechanized fog signal ringing every 15 seconds during low visibility. From 1876 to 1897, Fort Sumter was manned only by an ordnance sergeant and a lightkeeper. They lived at the fort with their families.

A modern interior view of Fort Sumter National Monument. *Photograph by Joe McLemore.*

An interior view of Fort Sumter National Monument showing the site of the former kitchen and magazine. *Photograph by Joe McLemore.*

International tension over Cuba's independence from Spain and the threat of war renewed concerns about coastal defense along the United States Atlantic coast. The guns at Fort Sumter, by 1895, were not operable and the site was in a general state of disrepair. Plans were developed in December 1895 to construct a concrete battery within the fort. In 1896, a new wharf was built for the fort and a 455-foot artisan well was dug to replace the cisterns for fresh water supply.

By 1898, construction began on a new concrete battery with two 12-inch rifled guns located on the fort's parade ground. The battery was named Battery Huger, in honor of General Isaac Huger, a Revolutionary War hero. Though the Spanish-American War ended in August 1898 with no combat on the American mainland, construction on Battery Huger and improvements to Fort Sumter

The flags displayed at the Fort Sumter National Monument. *Photograph by Joe McLemore.*

continued until December 31, 1899. In addition to the concrete battery, a two-story barracks to house 50 men and two-story ordnance sergeant's quarters were constructed. The fort's complex also housed the lighthouse, a bell tower, an oil house to store fuel for the Fresnel light, and the lightkeeper's house.

During World War I, a small garrison was stationed at Fort Sumter to man the guns at Battery Huger, though they never were involved in any action. There was little activity at Fort Sumter in the early twentieth century other than tourists who visited Charleston and booked boat transportation to see the fort where the Civil War began.

The two 12-inch guns at Battery Huger were removed for scrap in 1943, and replaced with two 90 mm antiaircraft guns manned by a company of the Coast Artillery.

In April 1948, Fort Sumter was designated as a National Monument and was transferred from the War Department to the National Park Service on July 12, 1948. In 1966, Fort Sumter was added to the National Register of Historic Places. Fort Sumter is open to the public and can be accessed by tour boats departing from both Charleston and Mount Pleasant. The Fort Sumter National Monument is visited by more than 270,000 people annually.

Fort Sumter as seen in 1903 from a boat in the harbor. *Courtesy of the Library of Congress.*

Peter Conover Hains

Peter Conover Hains, the son of a poor Philadelphia shoemaker, entered the United States Military Academy at West Point in 1857. His class graduated in June 1861, and produced 31 Union officers, 21 Confederate officers and nine generals. More than one-half of the class was killed in the Civil War.

Upon graduation, Hains was commissioned as a second lieutenant with the 2nd Artillery at Fort Meyer, Virginia. He was part of the Federal troops assembled for the First Battle of Bull Run and fired the Parrott rifle to signal the beginning of the attack.

Hains was later assigned as an engineer in the XIII Corps in the Union Army of Tennessee. After his superior fell ill, Hains assumed the task of General Ulysses Grant's chief engineer for the Siege of Vicksburg. Grant said of Hains, "Captain Hains is a most excellent officer and was recommended for the Colonelcy of a New Jersey regiment more than a year since." A monument to the honor of Chief Engineer Hains can be found on the grounds of the Vicksburg National Military Park in Mississippi.

This photograph, taken at Fair Oaks, Virginia, prior to the Battle of Bull Run, was of the brigade officers of the Horse Artillery commanded by Lieutenant Colonel William Hay. Lieutenant Hains is in the middle row, second from the left. *Courtesy of the Library of Congress.*

After the war, Hains accepted a position with the United States Lighthouse Service. As District Engineer for the 6th Lighthouse District, he supervised the construction of all the harbor lights in Charleston Harbor from the main lighthouse on Morris Island, to the smaller range lights, the lighthouse atop Fort Sumter, at the site of former Fort Ripley and ending in the steeple of St. Philip's Episcopal Church in Charleston.

In 1879, he transferred to the Army Corps of Engineers and designed the improvements to the Potomac River, turning a 650-acre foul-smelling swamp at Washington into the "Tidal Basin." Hains was also the engineer to mount a successful argument to build the canal in Panama.

During the Spanish-American War, Hains served as brigadier general of volunteers and commander of the Third Division of the First Corps. He was involved in the capture of Guayama and Las Palmas, Puerto Rico.

After the war, Hains returned to the Army Corps of Engineers and built the National Road from Washington to Mt. Vernon, today known as the George Washington Parkway. He became a prolific writer for magazines and military journals. In 1921, 20 years before the attack on Pearl Harbor, Hains wrote an article predicting an attack on the United States by the Empire of Japan to fulfill their need for oil.

Hains retired in 1904, but was reinstated as a major general in 1917 by the direction of the president and an act of Congress. He served as Chief Engineer of Norfolk Harbor and River District and commander of the defenses at Hampton Roads so a younger officer could serve in Europe for World War I. Hains was the only officer serving on active duty in the Civil War, the Spanish-American War and World War I.

Battery Huger

Battery Huger, constructed at Fort Sumter, was named for Isaac Huger, a planter and Continental Army general in the Revolutionary War. Huger was born on March 19, 1742, at Limerick Plantation on the Cooper River. The son of wealthy French Huguenot parents, he was educated in Europe.

He began his military career as a lieutenant with Colonel Thomas Middleton's Provincial South Carolina Regiment for service in the 1760 Cherokee campaign.

He was appointed a lieutenant colonel in the 1st South Carolina Regiment on June 17, 1775. On September 16, 1776, Huger was promoted to colonel, commanding the 5th South Carolina Regiment. On January 9, 1779, he was promoted to brigadier general in the Continental Army and fought in the major battles of the southern campaign.

Brigadier General Huger commanded the left wing of the Patriot Army at the Battle of Stono Ferry on June 20, 1779, where he was severely wounded. After recovering, he commanded the South Carolina and Georgia militia during the October 1779 Siege of Savannah. In the 1780 Siege of Charleston, Huger commanded a company of light dragoons and militia, but his company was defeated by British Colonel Banastre Tarleton at Monck's Corner on April 14, 1780. Due to an illness, he was not in Charleston when the city surrendered, saving him from capture. He later re-joined the Patriot Army with Major General Nathaniel Greene at the Battle of Cowpens and with General Horatio Gates in North Carolina, participating in the Battles of Guilford Court House and Hobkirk's Hill.

After the Revolutionary War, Huger was made vice president of the Society of the Cincinnati of the State of South Carolina, "founded to preserve the ideals and fellowship of the Revolutionary War officers." He represented St. George Dorchester in the South Carolina General Assembly from 1782 until his election as Sheriff of the Charleston District in 1785. In 1789, Huger was appointed by George Washington as the first Federal marshal for South Carolina, holding that office until 1793, when he resigned due to poor health. He died on October 17, 1797, in Charleston, at the age of 54.

Brigadier General Isaac Huger. *Courtesy of the Library of Congress.*

Commemorating the Sesquicentennial of the Civil War in Charleston

From 2010 – 2015, commemorative events will be held throughout the United States to recognize the 150th anniversary of the Civil War. Below is a listing of the major events of the war in Charleston and the dates of their 150th anniversaries. Information about Civil War events can be found at www.sc150civilwar.palmettohistory.org.

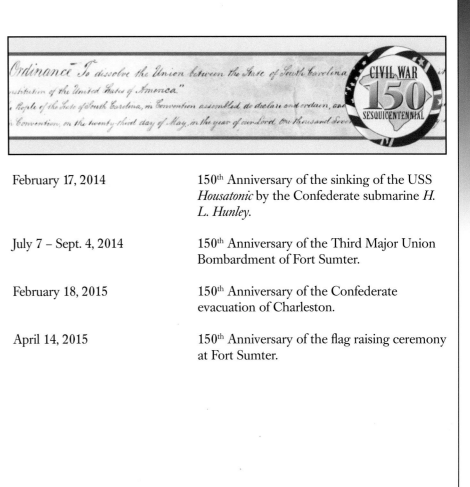

December 20, 2010	150th Anniversary of South Carolina's secession from the Union.
January 9, 2011	150th Anniversary of the firing on the *Star of the West* by Citadel cadets at Fort Morris on Morris Island.
April 12, 2011	150th Anniversary of the firing of the "First Shot," recognized as the beginning of the Civil War.
June 16, 2012	150th Anniversary of the Battle of Secessionville, James Island
January 30, 2013	150th Anniversary of the capture of the USS *Isaac Smith* by Confederates in the Stono River.
April 7, 2013	150th Anniversary of the ironclad attack on Fort Sumter
July 18, 2013	150th Anniversary of the Union assault on Battery Wagner, Morris Island.
Aug. 17 – Sept. 2, 2013	150th Anniversary of the First Major Union Bombardment of Fort Sumter.
Oct. 26 – Dec. 6, 2013	150th Anniversary of the Second Major Union Bombardment of Fort Sumter.
February 17, 2014	150th Anniversary of the sinking of the USS *Housatonic* by the Confederate submarine *H. L. Hunley*.
July 7 – Sept. 4, 2014	150th Anniversary of the Third Major Union Bombardment of Fort Sumter.
February 18, 2015	150th Anniversary of the Confederate evacuation of Charleston.
April 14, 2015	150th Anniversary of the flag raising ceremony at Fort Sumter.

Bibliography

Berhow, Mark A., editor. *American Seacoast Defenses: A Reference Guide*. New York: Coastal Defense Study Group Press, 2004.

Boatner III, Mark Mayo. *The Civil War Dictionary*. New York: McKay Publishing, 1959.

Bostick, Douglas W. *The Confederacy's Secret Weapon: Frank Vizetelly and the Illustrated London News*. Charleston: The History Press, 2009.

Bostick, Douglas W. *Secession to Siege: The Charleston Engravings*. Charleston: Joggling Board Press, 2004.

Bostick, Douglas W. *The Union is Dissolved! Charleston and Fort Sumter in the Civil War*. Charleston: The History Press, 2009.

Brennan, Patrick. *Secessionville: Assault on Charleston*. Savas Publishing Company, 1996.

Browning Jr., Robert M. *Success is all that was Expected: The South Atlantic Blockading Squadron during the Civil War*. Washington: Brassey's Inc., 2002.

Burton, E. Milby. *The Siege of Charleston: 1861- 1865*. Columbia: University of South Carolina Press, 1970.

Castel, Albert. *Fort Sumter: 1861*. Harrisburg, PA: Eastern Acorn Press, 1981.

Charleston Courier. Charleston, SC, 1860-61.

Coker III, P. C., *Charleston's Maritime Heritage, 1670-1865,* Charleston: CokerCraft Press, 1987.

Crawford, Samuel W. *The Genesis of the Civil War: The Story of Sumter, 1860-1861*. New York: Charles L. Webster and Company, 1887.

Cullum, George Washington. *Biographical Register of the Officers and Graduates of the United States Military Academy*. New York: Houghton, Mifflin, 1868.

Dahlgren, Madeline Vinton. *Memoir of John A. Dahlgren, Rear-Admiral of the United States Navy*. Boston, 1882.

Detzer, David. *Allegiance: Fort Sumter, Charleston and the Beginning of the Civil War*. New York: Harcourt, Inc., 2001.

Doubleday, Abner. *Reminiscences of Forts Sumter and Moultrie in 1860-61*. New York: Harper and Brothers, 1876.

Fort Sumter – Anvil of War (NPS Handbook 127). Washington, D. C.: U. S. Government Printing Office, 1984.

Frank Leslie's Illustrated Newspaper. New York, 1860-61.

French, Justus Clement and Edward Cary. *The trip of the steamer Oceanus to Fort Sumter and Charleston, S.C. Comprising the programme of exercises at the re-raising of the flag over the ruins of Fort Sumter, April 14th, 1865*. Brooklyn: The Union Steam Printing House, 1865.

Gilchrist, Major Robert. *The Confederate Defense of Morris Island, Charleston Harbor*. Charleston: New and Courier Book Presses, 1887.

Gilmore, Q. A. *Engineer and Artillery Operations Against the Defenses of Charleston Harbor*. New York, 1865.

_____. *Supplementary Engineer and Artillery Operations Against the Defenses of Charleston Harbor*. New York, 1868.

Harper's Weekly Journal of Civilization. New York, 1860-61.

Heyward, DuBose and Herbert R. Sass. *Fort Sumter, 1861-65.* New York, 1932.

Historic American Building Survey, Fort Sumter, HABS No. SC-194. Washington: Library of Congress.

Hoole, William Stanley. *Vizetelly Covers the Confederacy.* Tuscaloosa, AL: University of Alabama Press, 1957.

The Honour Letters, unpublished.

Illustrated London News. London, England, 1860-64.

Johnson, John. *The Defense of Charleston Harbor Including Fort Sumter and the Adjacent Sea Islands, 1863 -1865.* Charleston: Walker, Evans, and Cogswell, 1890.

Jones, Samuel. *The Siege of Charleston and the Operations on the South Atlantic Coast in the War Among the States.* New York: The Neale Publishing Company, 1911.

Klein, Maury. *Days of Defiance: Sumter, Secession and the Coming of the Civil War.* New York: Vintage Books, 1999.

Lawton, Eba Anderson. *Major Robert Anderson and Fort Sumter 1861.* New York: The Knickerbocker Press, 1911.

Lebby, Robert, Jr., MD. *The First Shot on Fort Sumter.* South Carolina Historical and Genealogical Magazine, July 1911.

McGovern, Terrance and Belling Smith. *American Coastal Defenses, 1885 – 1950.* New York: Osprey Publishing, 2006.

Mellichamp, Robert Elliott, *Sketch of James Island*, unpublished, 1888. *Mercury.* Charleston, SC, 1860-61.

Minutes of the Washington Light Infantry, Charleston, SC.

Roman, Alfred. *The Military Operations of General Beauregard in the War Between the States, 1861 to 1865.* New York: Harper and Brothers, 1883.

Schreadley, R. L. *Valor and Virtue: The Washington Light Infantry in Peace and In War.* Spartanburg, SC: The Reprint Publishers, 1997.

"The Slave Ship and Slave Cargo at Charleston." The New York Times, September 6, 1858.

"Special Orders # 62", *Charleston Mercury*, May 2, 1863.

"Stories of a Confederate," *The National Magazine,* Volume X, April 1899 – September 1899, pages 41-54.

Swansburg, W. A. *First Blood: The Story of Fort Sumter.* New York: Charles Scribner's Sons, 1957.

US Department of Commerce, Bureau of the Census, "South Carolina 1860 Federal Census," Washington, DC: Government Printing Office, Microfilm Copy.

_____, Bureau of the Census, "South Carolina 1860 Federal Slave Census," Washington, DC: Government Printing Office, Microfilm Copy.

_____, Bureau of the Census, "South Carolina 1860 Federal Agricultural Census," Washington, DC: Government Printing Office, Microfilm Copy.

War of the Rebellion: A Compilation of the Official Records of the Union and Confederate Armies. Washington, D.C.: U. S. Government Printing Office, 1880 - 1901.

Wilcox, Arthur M. and Warren Ripley. *The Civil War at Charleston.* Charleston: The Evening Post Publishing Company, 1966.

Wise, Stephen, R. *Gate of Hell: Campaign for Charleston Harbor, 1863.* Columbia: University of South Carolina Press, 1994.